COOKING WITH THE
Chicken Man

COOKING WITH THE
Chicken Man

LEONARD THOMAS

WARNER BOOKS

A Time Warner Company

Warner Books, Inc., 1271 Avenue of the Americas, New York, NY 10020
Visit our Web site at http://warnerbooks.com

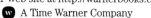 A Time Warner Company

Printed in the United States of America
First Printing: August 1998
10 9 8 7 6 5 4 3 2 1

LIBRARY OF CONGRESS CATALOGING-IN-PUBLICATION DATA
Thomas, Leonard
    Cooking with the chicken man / Leonard Thomas.
        p.   cm.
    Includes index.
    ISBN 0-446-67376-5
    1. Cookery (Chicken)   I. Title.
TX750.5.C45T48   1998
641.6'65—dc21   97-51974
                                                  CIP

Interior photographs by Nancy Palubniak
Cartoons by R. J. Matson
Illustrations by Giorgetta McRee
Book design by Kathryn Parise
Cover design by Jon Valk
Cover photo by Nancy Palubniak

To my uncle, Frank Shervington

ACKNOWLEDGMENTS

First, I would like to thank God, without whom I would not have been able to write this book and make these changes in my life. Next, I would like to thank my wife, Yvette, for saying yes when I asked her to marry me, and I want to thank her daughter, Anika, for finding me. (Anika and my nephew, Kevin, brought us together on a blind date.) Thanks and love to my parents, Thelma and Henry Thomas, because without them there would not be a Chicken Man. Thanks and love to the rest of my family and all my friends who support me. Thanks to my supervisors and co-workers for listening to me talk about chicken all day and being guinea pigs for some of my recipes—I know that must have driven you all crazy! Thanks to Vera Moore Cosmetics for allowing me to represent them at my first charity function, and to the two teachers who inspired me the most, Chef Belinda and Chef Roberts. Thanks to Ann Tripp and her radio friends for eating my chicken on the air, and to the journalists Randy Kennedy and Chester Higgins, Jr., for seeing more than a city worker on a bridge. Thanks to my manager, Renee Harriston, for all her good advice, my editor, Amye Dyer, for seeing the potential in me and not giving up, and the others who helped make this book happen—Diane Luger, Nancy Palubniak, and R. J. Matson.

I would like to take this opportunity to publicly thank the New York City Department of Transportation, Bureau of Bridges, for allowing me the time, space, and positive cooperation in writing my cookbook.

I would especially like to thank Mr. William F. Chasse, director of bridges, for his encouragement and latitude.

CONTENTS

INTRODUCTION

I'M JUST AN ORDINARY GUY who works for the city's Department of Transportation raising the drawbridges so the barges and boats can pass. I've been working on one New York City bridge or another for the past twenty-two years—from the Harlem River Bridge to the Gowanus Canal to my current post at the Union Street Bridge in Park Slope, Brooklyn. Now, working the bridges won't make you rich, but it does give you the opportunity to meet a lot of interesting people and because of the decrease in waterway traffic in past years there is often a lot of time to think. Some days I'm hopping—opening and closing that drawbridge nonstop, and some days I'm just sitting there for what seems like forever and waiting for something, *anything,* to happen. I could talk forever about all my varied experiences on the bridges (I'll save that for another book!), but the most important, the one I want to tell you about now, is the story of how I became known as the Chicken Man.

A good friend of mine, Raven the Cake Man of Harlem, got his name because he makes the most fantastic cakes you have ever tasted. One afternoon about four years ago, I took one of my stuffed chickens over to Raven because I knew he was hungry for a good meal. After a couple of bites, he gave me a big smile and said, "This is good chicken. I'm gonna start calling you the Chicken Man. I'm the Cake Man and you're the Chicken Man." Well, that's how the name came about, but it's really just the beginning.

I love chicken. I think about chicken and recipe ideas just pop into my head: fried chicken, grilled chicken, barbecued chicken, roasted chicken, Cajun chicken, tandoori chicken, chicken and rice, sautéed chicken, and my specialty, deboned chicken stuffed with wild rice, collard greens, and turkey sausage—I love them all. After years of raising the bridge and thinking about chicken, I decided to get serious about cooking. My wife provided the nudge when she gave me an eleven-week course at the French Culinary Institute in New York City as a wedding gift (on our first date I cooked for her, and you could say the rest is history). I've always felt at home in the kitchen and I was in my glory standing alongside Jacques Pepin, Chef Roberts, and Chef Belinda day to day—chopping, deboning, sautéing, and baking. I was inspired—what had once been just a hobby I wanted to turn into a part-time career. After I completed the course, I started Lenny's Stuffed Chickens—a one-man operation—serving chicken all over New York City. But I still work the bridges and the catering is done on my days off and weekends.

While working on one of the city's busiest bridges—the Mill Basin Bridge—I often called up the guys at one of the local radio stations to report any activity or traffic mishaps. These guys were great, so one day I decided to take them some of my special chicken wrapped in foil. They must have liked it because next thing I know they're asking me to call in every now and then to talk about traffic *and* chicken. After a while, some listeners who heard me on the radio were saying, "Hey, Chicken Man, what's up?" People I didn't even know were starting to call me the Chicken Man. But the real validation for the Chicken Man occurred when my face and story landed on the front page of the Metro section of the *New York Times*. Now, everybody who read that article was calling me the Chicken

Man and doors were opening. It was time for the Chicken Man to make his move. Who would have ever thought that cooking on those little stoves on the bridge would turn me into the Chicken Man? Wow!

Here's an example of how my two worlds—the bridge and chicken—are forever intertwined (and I wouldn't have it any other way). The average day shift for a bridge worker is eight hours, and the night shift is sixteen. For the last ten years I've worked the day shift, and occasionally I'll get stuck working my shift *and* someone else's. That makes for a very long day, but over the years I've mastered some of the best fried, stuffed, grilled, boiled, broiled, steamed, sautéed, poached, and roasted chicken that you can lay your lips on, and the aroma—it just dances in your nose. (Getting hungry?) Believe it or not, one Saturday while working the Mill Basin Bridge in Brooklyn, I decided to take my smoker to work to smoke a few chickens. On Saturdays during the summer, the car traffic is heavy because we have to open the bridge for so many sailboats. So this guy, sitting in his car, rolled down the window and said, "That smells good. What is it?"

I said, "Smoked chicken."

"Man, can I buy one of those chickens from you?"

"Get out of here, I'm not selling these chickens."

The guy was persistent. He kept after me, saying he had a party to go to that evening and needed to bring a dish. By this time he's holding up a line of cars, causing a traffic jam, so to get rid of the guy I sold him the chicken, pan and all, for $15. In my mind I pretty much kissed that pan good-bye, but the next day he's back, returning the pan, and raving about my smoked chicken. Since then I've catered a few of his parties, including his daughter's christening!

I have a specialty, and that specialty is deboned chicken. A lot of people cringe at the word *deboned;* they think it's too difficult. It's not, but it is becoming a lost culinary art. Follow the easy instructions on page 6, or if you don't want to debone the chicken yourself, ask your local butcher to help you out; I promise it's worth it. The possibilities with a deboned chicken are limitless; you can stuff it with anything you want—a favorite of mine is Chicken Stuffed with Yellow Rice and Shrimp (page 134). (Getting hungrier?)

To me, chicken is the universal language. I can talk about chicken to anyone at any time. Everyone has a good chicken recipe that has been handed down from a mother, grandmother, uncle, or brother—a family history that should be treasured and not forgotten. My love of good food and cooking for people has opened doors that I never knew existed, and for that I'm thankful because I get to do what I love doing—and that's cooking chicken. Let's eat!

CHICKEN MAN'S KITCHEN ESSENTIALS

boning knife

chef's knife

carving knife and fork

poultry shears

stockpot

frying pan

casserole

sauté pan

roasting pan and rack

13 × 9 × 2-inch rectangular baking dish

8½ × 4-inch loaf pan

meat thermometer

acrylic cutting boards (This type of board is nonporous and the least likely to harbor bacteria.)

wooden spoons

mixing bowl

colander

measuring spoons and cups

metal tongs

meat mallet

pot holders

skimmer

basting brush

basting bulb

kitchen string

grill baskets for barbecuing

DO YOU KNOW YOUR CHICKENS?

BROILER-FRYER: Tender, all-purpose chicken that ranges from 1½ to 3½ pounds. About 9 to 12 weeks old, it contains the least fat.

ROASTER: Chicken weight between 3½ to 5 pounds and 3 to 5 months old. The meat is tender and should be roasted or grilled because of the fat content.

CAPON: A rooster that has been castrated at a young age and fed a special fattening diet. Ranging from 4 to 9 pounds, a capon has large quantities of tender, juicy breast meat. It is great for roasting.

STEWING: This chicken (also referred to as a hen) weighs 4½ to 6 pounds and provides a generous amount of meat. It is a mature, less tender bird and is best cooked by simmering or in stews and soups.

ROCK CORNISH HEN: This small, young, specially bred chicken (also referred to as a game hen) weighs 1 to 1½ pounds and has all white meat. Allow one per person.

WHEN YOU ARE ROASTING CHICKEN IN THE OVEN, ON A RACK, ALWAYS ADD ¼ CUP WATER TO THE PAN, WHICH WILL KEEP THE SMOKE DOWN DURING COOKING. IT ALSO KEEPS THE CHICKEN MOIST.

How to Debone a Chicken

1. Remove the giblets. Rinse the chicken under cold water and pat dry. Lay the chicken on a sturdy surface or cutting board, breast side down. Cut along the backbone from neck to tail.

2. Remove the wishbone. It is located just under the surface of the neck.

3. Along the backbone, begin cutting and scraping away from the ribcage. Keep the knife close to the bones. Cut to the thigh and wing on both sides.

Cut until you expose the thigh bone socket. Insert the knife in the socket, freeing the bone. Repeat on the other side.

Cut the ribcage free. Locate the area where the rib bones meet the breastbone and slice there.

4. Find the curved bone near the wing. Slice next to the bone, then cut down to the joint. Cut through the joint to remove the bone.

Scrape and cut around the breastbone. Separate the cartilage from the meat.

Cut all the way around the first joint of the wing down to the bone. Remove the wing on both sides. Refrigerate the chicken until ready to use.

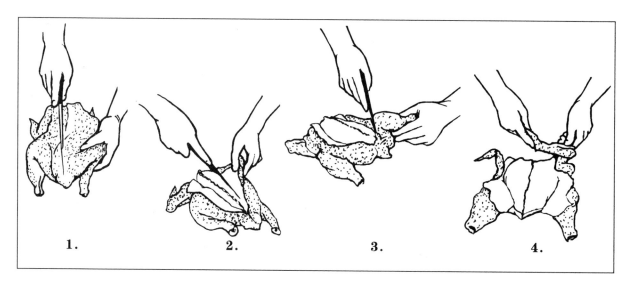

1.   2.   3.   4.

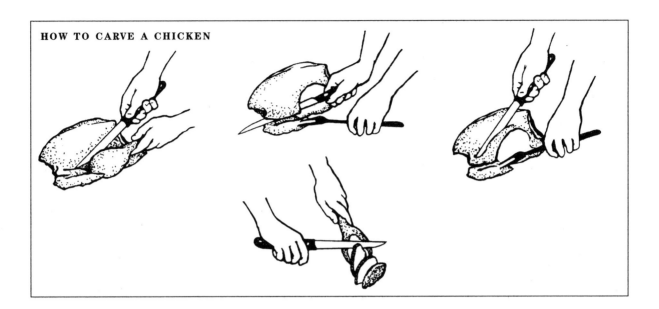

HOW TO CARVE A CHICKEN

Stuffing a Deboned Chicken

Lay the chicken skin side down. Salt and pepper the entire surface. Place 1½ to 2 cups of stuffing into cavity.

Start at the tail end and fold the sides together. Tuck the cut end underneath. Fold the neck flap over *last* to seal.

Secure the neck and tail flap with skewers or toothpicks. Secure in the middle.

Use string to lace through the skewers. Cross the chicken legs and wrap the string around several times to secure. Tie off the string. Finished!

WHY SHOULD YOU LET CHICKEN REST BEFORE CARVING? IT IS BEST TO LET CHICKEN REST 5 TO 10 MINUTES BEFORE CARVING BECAUSE THE MEAT NEEDS TO RELAX SO THAT THE FLESH WILL NOT TEAR. USE A SHARP CARVING KNIFE AND WORK ON A STEADY SURFACE.

HOW TO CUT CHICKEN INTO 12 PIECES

THIS IS THE BEST WAY TO FRY CHICKEN BECAUSE ALL THE PIECES WILL COOK EVENLY.

12 PIECES

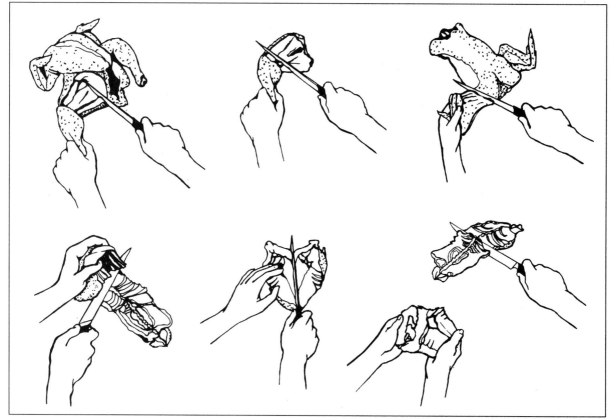

BUYING CHICKEN

One thing that is very important to me is the quality of the chicken I eat. There are many brands out there, but no matter what brand of chicken you buy always check the sell-by date. Also check the amount of liquid that is in the bag or tray the chicken is packaged in; there should be very little to none.

Hey, just like you should avoid buying dented cans, avoid buying packages that are torn and leaking. Check for any odor; don't be afraid to put that package to your nose and smell. Remember, you are buying it to eat.

 MAKE CLEANLINESS A PRIORITY IN YOUR KITCHEN. ALWAYS THOROUGHLY WASH CUTTING BOARDS, KNIVES, AND ANY OTHER SURFACES THAT HAVE COME IN CONTACT WITH RAW CHICKEN. (WE HAVE A DEAL IN OUR HOUSE—WHOEVER COOKS GETS TO PROP THEIR FEET UP WHILE SOMEONE ELSE DOES THE DISHES!)

ROASTING TIMES BASED ON WEIGHT

3 pounds	50 to 55 minutes @ 375°F
3½ pounds	55 to 60 minutes @ 375°F
4 pounds	60 to 65 minutes @ 375°F
4½ pounds	60 to 65 minutes @ 375°F

CHICKEN HOT LINE

FOR ANSWERS TO YOUR QUESTIONS ABOUT CHICKEN HANDLING OR SAFETY, CALL THE UNITED STATES DEPARTMENT OF AGRICULTURE'S MEAT AND POULTRY HOT LINE.

THE TOLL-FREE NUMBER IS (800) 535-4555. (IN THE WASHINGTON, D.C., AREA, CALL (202) 477-3333.)

HOME ECONOMISTS AT THE HOT LINE TAKE CALLS FROM 10 A.M. TO 4 P.M. EASTERN STANDARD TIME, WITH EXTENDED HOURS DURING THE MONTH OF NOVEMBER.

HOW TO TELL WHEN CHICKEN IS DONE

Insert a meat thermometer into the thickest part of the chicken. The temperature should register around 170°F. to 180°F.

On a whole chicken, the legs will move easily in their sockets when done.

When the chicken is pricked with a knife, the juices should run clear.

Boneless chicken will be opaque and white throughout with no traces of pink.

SHAKESPEARE AND THE EGG TEST

O, now doest thou knowest when thine eggs are
  fresh?
Place in water for this simple test.
If thine eggs are standing and erect, you can bet
  thine eggs are a mess.
But if thine eggs are lying at the bottom when you
  do this, o, yes, my lord, thine eggs are fresh.

STARTERS

THE-DEVIL-MADE-ME-DO-IT EGGS

It seems appropriate to begin this book with a recipe that pays homage to the age-old question: Which came first—the chicken or the egg?

12 **large eggs**
 5 **tablespoons mayonnaise**
 1 **tablespoon Dijon mustard**
   Freshly ground black pepper
   Old Bay Seasoning
 1 **4½-ounce can medium
   shrimp**
   Paprika

Place the eggs in a large pot, cover with cold water, and bring to a boil. Lower the heat to a simmer and cook about 13 minutes; drain. Rinse the eggs under cold running water until they are cool enough to handle.

Shell the eggs and cut in halves lengthwise. Place the yolks in a food processor with the mayonnaise and mustard and process until well blended. Remove the yolk mixture from the processor and place in a bowl. Season to taste with pepper and Old Bay Seasoning. Set aside 24 shrimp. Finely chop the remaining shrimp and fold into the yolk mixture. Spoon into the egg whites, place 1 shrimp on top of each, and sprinkle with paprika.

Serves 10 to 12

98.7 KISS FM

One morning, while on my way to work, I was listening to Ann Tripp reporting the traffic. She said that there had been a car accident at the Mill Basin Bridge, and that traffic was at a standstill. However, where I was, the traffic was moving just fine. When I arrived at the bridge, I asked a co-worker about the accident and he just gave me a look that said that I was nuts! I turned the radio on and Ann Tripp was still reporting this incident, so I decided to call the station to correct her.

The night guard answered the telephone. I told him that there had *not* been a car accident on the bridge and he said, "I'll let you tell Ann Tripp." I told her who I was and that there was no accident. She asked, "How do you know?" I responded that I work on the Mill Basin Bridge and that I make the best chicken in New York. They call me the Chicken Man!

After that, I started calling the station to give Ann the traffic conditions across my bridge. One day Ann teasingly asked, "You talk about how good your chicken is, well, how do we know?" I decided to take her up on the dare so I went to the station with four chickens: two deboned and stuffed with wild rice, collard greens, and sausage; the other two stuffed with yellow rice and shrimp. After Ann Tripp and the Wake Up Club tasted my chicken, we became good friends. That morning all the New York listeners and Ann Tripp fell for my chicken!

ANN TRIPP TERRIFIC TRAFFIC CHICKEN WINGS

2 pounds chicken wings (12 wings), disjointed
Salt and freshly ground black pepper
Vegetable oil for frying
1 teaspoon cornstarch
1 teaspoon cold water
1 14-ounce can pineapple chunks
2 tablespoons Grand Marnier

Wash the chicken wings and pat them dry; discard the wing tips. Season to taste with salt and pepper. In a heavy pot, heat the oil to 375°F. Place a few wings at a time in the oil and cook until golden brown and crisp, about 10 minutes. Drain on paper towels. When all the wings are cooked and drained, place in a large bowl. In a small cup, mix the cornstarch and cold water together and set aside. Drain the juice from the pineapple into a small saucepan, add the Grand Marnier, and bring to a boil. Add the cornstarch mixture and stir until thickened. Remove from the heat and pour over the chicken wings. Toss to coat. Add the pineapple chunks.

Serves 4 to 6

WINGS THAT WILL MAKE A BUFFALO CRY

One afternoon I was at a restaurant with a few buddies of mine. We were in the mood for something nice and spicy so we ordered the Buffalo wings. The wings they brought out were okay, but they weren't hot enough for my taste. So I decided to make up my own recipe. These wings would be so hot they would make that damn buffalo cry!

Vegetable oil for frying
2 pounds chicken wings (12 wings)
½ cup (1 stick) unsalted butter
¼ cup Trappey's West Indian–style hot sauce
1 teaspoon Tabasco
½ teaspoon paprika
Hellmann's Creamy Blue Cheese Dressing, or your favorite brand

Heat the oil to 375°F. in a deep-fryer or heavy saucepan. Disjoint the chicken wings; cut the wing tips off and discard. In a small saucepan, melt the butter. Add the hot sauce, Tabasco, and paprika and set aside. Deep-fry the wings about 8 to 12 minutes, or until golden brown and crisp. Drain on paper towels.

Place the wings in a large bowl, pour the hot sauce mixture on, and toss to coat the wings. Serve warm with blue cheese dipping sauce and celery. Some ice-cold beer wouldn't hurt either.

Serves 4 to 6

OWEN'S PLAIN OL' BAKED WINGS

One afternoon my co-worker Owen and I were talking chicken—dishing about some of our favorite recipes. The next day Owen brought in these wonderful wings.

2 **pounds whole chicken wings (12 wings)**
¼ **teaspoon salt, or to taste**
¼ **teaspoon freshly ground black pepper, or to taste**
½ **tablespoon dried parsley**
2 **tablespoons (¼ stick) unsalted butter, melted**
⅓ **cup water**

Preheat the oven to 350°F.

Place the chicken wings in a large bowl and season with the salt, pepper, parsley, and melted butter. Mix well; set aside for 1 hour. Add the water to a baking pan, place the wings in a single layer, and bake 15 minutes. Then turn the wings and bake another 15 minutes, or until they are crisp on the outside and tender inside.

Serves 4 to 6

OWEN'S WINGS WITH A LITTLE JAZZ

But of course I couldn't resist adding some spice.

2 **pounds whole chicken wings (12 wings)**
¼ **teaspoon salt, or to taste**
¼ **teaspoon freshly ground black pepper, or to taste**
½ **teaspoon paprika**
1 **garlic clove, minced**
1 **tablespoon dried parsley**
2 **tablespoons (¼ stick) unsalted butter, melted**
⅓ **cup white wine**

Preheat the oven to 350°F.

Place the chicken wings in a large bowl and season with the salt, pepper, paprika, garlic, and parsley. Pour on the melted butter and mix well; set aside for 1 hour. Add the white wine to a baking dish, place the wings in a single layer, and bake 15 minutes. Then turn and bake another 15 minutes, or until the wings are crisp on the outside and tender inside.

Serves 4 to 6

SWEET ORANGE WINGS

2 pounds chicken wings
(12 wings)
½ cup (1 stick) unsalted
butter, melted
1 10-ounce jar orange
marmalade
2 tablespoons Grand Marnier
1 tablespoon dark brown
sugar

Preheat the oven to 350°F.

Place the chicken wings on a foil-lined baking sheet and brush with melted butter. In a small bowl, mix half the jar of marmalade, the Grand Marnier, and brown sugar. (If the orange mixture is hard to mix, place in a microwave on low for a few seconds.) Bake the wings about 30 minutes, then remove from the oven and brush with the mixture. Return to the oven for 5 minutes, or until the wings are crisp.

Serves 4 to 6

JERK WINGS

Now, I can give you a recipe for making jerk seasoning, but like I told you from the start, some of us suffer from recipe phobia. So just go to your supermarket and in the Jamaican section you will find jerk seasoning. I use Walker's Wood Jerk Seasoning. It's delicious and the ingredients are all natural.

**3 pounds chicken wings
  (18 wings), disjointed
2 heaping tablespoons jerk
  seasoning, Walker's Wood
  or any other brand
⅓ cup dark rum**

Place the chicken wings in a large bowl; discard the tips. Add the jerk seasoning and rum and work into the wings with your hands. Cover and let marinate overnight in the refrigerator.

Preheat the broiler. Arrange the wings in a single layer on a pan, place 6 to 7 inches under the broiler, and cook about 7 minutes per side, or until the wings are done.

Serves 4 to 6

GINGER ALE CHICKEN NUGGETS

Vegetable oil for frying
1 **cup all-purpose flour**
1 **teaspoon salt**
½ **teaspoon freshly ground
    black pepper**
¼ **teaspoon paprika**
¾ **cup ginger ale**
1½ **pounds skinless, boneless
    chicken breast or thighs,
    cut into 1-inch chunks**

Heat the oil to 375°F. in a deep-fryer or heavy fry pan.

In a medium bowl, mix together the flour, salt, pepper, paprika, and ginger ale until smooth. Dip the chicken, one piece at a time, into the batter, coating completely. Shake off any excess batter. Carefully add to the hot oil and fry about 7 to 10 minutes, or until golden brown, turning once with tongs or a slotted spoon. Drain on paper towels.

Serves 4 to 6

BEER BATTER CHICKEN NUGGETS

Vegetable oil for frying
1 **cup all-purpose flour**
1 **teaspoon salt**
½ **teaspoon freshly ground black pepper**
¼ **teaspoon paprika**
Pinch of cayenne
¾ **cup beer**
1½ **pounds skinless, boneless chicken breast or thighs, cut into 1-inch chunks**

Heat the oil to 375°F in a deep-fryer or a heavy fry pan.

In a medium bowl, mix together the flour, salt, pepper, paprika, cayenne, and beer until smooth. Dip the chicken, one piece at a time, into the batter, coating completely. Shake off any excess batter. Carefully add to the hot oil and fry about 7 to 10 minutes, or until golden brown, turning once with tongs or a slotted spoon. Drain on paper towels.

Serves 4 to 6

BARBECUE CHICKEN BALLS

1 pound ground chicken

1½ pounds Italian pork sausage
  meat

2 tablespoons tomato paste

½ cup finely chopped onion

1 teaspoon liquid smoke

¼ teaspoon garlic powder

⅛ teaspoon salt, or to taste

⅛ teaspoon freshly ground
  black pepper

1 28-ounce bottle barbecue
  sauce

Preheat the oven to 350°F. In a large bowl, combine all the ingredients except the barbecue sauce. Mix well. Shape into small balls and place on a baking pan. Bake 20 minutes, then pour off any fat. Generously pour on the barbecue sauce and continue baking about 15 minutes more.

Serves 10 to 12 as an appetizer

CHUNKY CHICKEN SALAD

2½ cups cooked chicken, cut
   into chunks
¼ cup finely chopped red
   pepper
¼ cup finely chopped green
   pepper
1 celery stalk, finely chopped
½ cup finely chopped red
   onion
1 cup mayonnaise
2 tablespoons prepared
   mustard
   Salt and freshly ground
   black pepper to taste
   Shredded lettuce
   Sliced tomatoes

In a large bowl, combine all the ingredients except the lettuce and tomatoes. Serve on a bed of shredded lettuce with the sliced tomatoes.

Serves 4

CHICKEN MAN'S CHICKEN SALAD

2 cups chopped cooked
   chicken
1½ cups finely chopped celery
1 dill pickle, finely chopped
2 hard-boiled eggs, coarsely
   chopped
½ small red onion, finely
   chopped
3 tablespoons mayonnaise or
   more
Salt and freshly ground
   black pepper to taste

In a medium bowl, mix all the ingredients. Serve on a bed of shredded lettuce or as a sandwich filling.

Serves 4

FRIED CHICKEN

SPICY FRIED CHICKEN

This recipe appeared in the Metro section of the New York Times.

1 **3-pound chicken, cut into serving pieces**
½ **teaspoon salt**
½ **teaspoon freshly ground black pepper**
¼ **teaspoon garlic powder**
¼ **teaspoon onion powder**
1 **cup all-purpose flour**
¼ **cup Old Bay Seasoning**
1 **teaspoon cayenne**
1 **large egg**
2 **tablespoons water**
2 **cups vegetable or peanut oil**

Wash the chicken and pat it dry. In a large bowl, combine the chicken, salt, black pepper, and garlic and onion powders. Rub the spices in well. In a large paper or plastic bag, mix the flour, Old Bay Seasoning, and cayenne. In a medium bowl, beat the egg and water until well blended. Dip the chicken pieces in the egg mixture, then place in the bag with the flour and shake to coat. Repeat with the remaining chicken.

In a 12-inch skillet, heat the oil to 350°F. Add the chicken, skin side down, and cover. After 5 minutes, uncover; the pan should remain uncovered for the remaining time. After 5 more minutes, turn all the pieces over. Continue cooking for about 10 minutes, or until well browned and crisp and the juices run clear. Remove the chicken to paper towels. Let sit for 5 minutes and serve.

Serves 6

WHEN YOU MIX ANY KIND OF SEASONING WITH FLOUR, YOU SHOULD TASTE THE FLOUR FOR FLAVOR. WET THE TIP OF YOUR FINGER, DAB A LITTLE FLOUR ON THAT FINGER, AND TASTE.

MAMA'S FRIED CHICKEN

1   **3-pound chicken, cut into serving pieces**
1   **cup all-purpose flour**
1   **teaspoon salt**
1   **teaspoon freshly ground black pepper**
1   **teaspoon garlic powder**
¼   **teaspoon cayenne**
2   **tablespoons paprika**
2   **cups Crisco shortening for frying**

Wash the chicken and pat it dry. In a large plastic or brown paper bag, mix the flour, salt, pepper, garlic powder, cayenne, and paprika. Put a few pieces of chicken in the bag and shake to coat. Shake off any excess flour. Repeat with the remaining chicken.

In a 12-inch skillet, heat the shortening to 350°F. Add the chicken, skin side down, and cover. After 5 minutes, uncover; the pan should remain uncovered for the remaining time. After 5 more minutes, turn all the chicken pieces over. Continue cooking for about 10 minutes, or until well browned and crisp and the juices run clear when pricked with a fork. Remove the chicken to paper towels. Let sit for 5 minutes and serve.

Serves 4 to 6

FRIED CHICKEN WITH A LITTLE ZEST

1 **3-pound chicken, cut into serving pieces**
1½ **teaspoons lemon pepper**
1 **teaspoon lemon juice**
1 **cup all-purpose flour**
½ **tablespoon paprika**
   Vegetable oil for frying
   Zest of ½ lemon, as garnish

Season the chicken with 1 teaspoon of lemon pepper and the lemon juice, put into a zip lock bag, and marinate in the refrigerator for 1 hour or overnight. In a plastic or brown paper bag, mix the flour, paprika, and remaining ½ teaspoon of lemon pepper. Put a few pieces of chicken in the bag and shake to coat. Shake off any excess flour. Repeat with the remaining chicken.

In a 12-inch skillet, heat the oil to 350°F. Add the chicken, skin side down, and cover. After 5 minutes, uncover; the pan should remain uncovered for the remaining time. After 5 more minutes, turn all the pieces over. Continue cooking for 10 minutes, or until well browned and crisp. Remove the chicken to paper towels. Let sit for 5 minutes. Garnish with lemon zest and serve.

Serves 4 to 6

BUBBA'S BEST FRIED CHICKEN

Bubba is one of my cooking buddies. When other men are talking about cars, women, and football, we are talking about food. After Bubba vacationed in Virginia, he came back with this great recipe.

1   **3-pound chicken, cut into serving pieces**
1   **cup all-purpose flour**
1   **teaspoon salt**
½   **teaspoon freshly ground black pepper**
½   **tablespoon paprika**
1   **teaspoon poultry seasoning**
¾   **cup vegetable oil**
⅓   **cup bacon drippings**

Preheat the oven to 350°F. Wash the chicken and pat it dry.

In a plastic or brown paper bag, mix the flour, salt, pepper, paprika, and poultry seasoning. Put a few pieces of chicken in the bag and shake to coat. Shake off any excess flour.

In a 12-inch skillet, heat the oil and bacon drippings over medium-high heat. Brown the chicken, then put in a baking dish and cover with aluminum foil. Bake about 30 minutes, uncover, and continue baking for 15 minutes, or until the chicken is tender and the juices run clear.

Serves 4

BUTTERMILK FRIED CHICKEN

The first time I went down South was in the '70s. I went with a schoolmate who was meeting his fiancée's parents for the first time (I was going to be the best man at his wedding). The thing I remember most about this trip was the food—it was the first time I was exposed to real *southern cooking.*

The first morning, when I walked into the kitchen for breakfast, I had to stop and take a deep breath. When I saw the amount of food on the table, I thought I had died and gone to "food heaven." There were eggs, bacon, pork chops, sausage, fried chicken, fish, grits, rice, ham, fried apples, biscuits, home-fried potatoes, gravy, milk, orange juice, and freshly brewed coffee. I will never forget the spread of food on that table, and all the while they were asking me if I had enough to eat! I couldn't move. The buttermilk fried chicken was delicious and one of the first recipes in my collection. This was my first taste of southern hospitality and man, was it nice.

1 **3-pound chicken, cut into serving pieces**
1 **cup buttermilk**
½ **teaspoon salt**
½ **teaspoon coarse black pepper**
1 **cup all-purpose flour**
1 **tablespoon paprika**
2 **cups Crisco vegetable shortening for frying**

Wash the chicken and pat it dry. In a bowl, combine the chicken, buttermilk, salt, and pepper. Marinate in the refrigerator for 1 hour. In a large plastic or brown paper bag, mix the flour, paprika, and salt and pepper to taste. Put a few pieces of chicken in the bag and shake to coat. Repeat with the remaining chicken. Shake off any excess flour. Place the chicken on a baking rack until time to cook.

In a 12-inch skillet, heat ½ inch vegetable shortening to 350°F. Add the chicken, skin side down, and cover. After 5 minutes, uncover; the pan should remain uncovered for the remaining time. After 5 more minutes, turn all the pieces over. Continue cooking about 10 minutes, or until well browned and crisp and the juices run clear. Remove the chicken to paper towels. Let sit for 5 minutes and serve.

Serves 4 to 6

ANIKA'S FRIED CHICKEN

I was in Atlanta, Georgia, visiting my stepdaughter, Anika, when one night for dinner she cooked this terrific fried chicken—it was crisp, juicy, and delicious. The recipe was very simple, but the flour she used, White Lily flour, is available only in the South. But see page 40 for the White Lily address.

1 **cup milk**
1 **3-pound chicken, cut into serving pieces**
   Salt and freshly ground black pepper
1 **cup White Lily flour**
2 **tablespoons paprika**
1 **teaspoon poultry seasoning**
   Vegetable or canola oil for frying

Wash the chicken and pat it dry. In a medium bowl, combine the milk and chicken. Season to taste with salt and pepper and set aside for 30 minutes. In a large brown paper or plastic bag, combine the flour, paprika, 1 teaspoon salt, ½ teaspoon pepper, and the poultry seasoning. Put a few pieces of chicken in the bag and shake to coat. Repeat with the remaining chicken. Shake off any excess flour.

In a 12-inch skillet, heat ½ inch of oil to 350°F. Add the chicken, skin side down, and cover. After 5 minutes, uncover; the pan should remain uncovered for the remaining time. After 5 more minutes, turn all the pieces over. Continue cooking for about 10 minutes, or until well browned and crisp and the juices run clear. Remove the chicken to paper towels. Let stand 5 minutes and serve.

Serves 4

MESQUITE FRIED CHICKEN

1 **3-pound chicken, cut into serving pieces**
   Salt and freshly ground pepper
1 **cup all-purpose flour**
2 to 3 **tablespoons Tone's Butter Mesquite Seasoning (see Note)**
   Vegetable or canola oil for frying

Wash the chicken and pat it dry. Season the chicken with salt and pepper. In a plastic or brown paper bag, combine the flour and Tone's Butter Mesquite Seasoning. Put a few pieces of chicken in the bag and shake to coat. Repeat with the remaining chicken. Shake off any excess flour

In a 12-inch skillet, heat ½ inch of oil to 350°F. Add the chicken, skin side down, and cover. After 5 minutes, uncover; the pan should remain uncovered for the remaining time. After 5 more minutes, turn all the pieces over. Continue cooking for about 10 minutes, or until well browned and crisp and the juices run clear. Remove the chicken to paper towels. Let sit for 5 minutes and serve.

Serves 4

NOTE: Tone's Butter Mesquite Seasoning is available at BJ's and Price Costco wholesale clubs, and your local supermarket. If you can't find it, call 1-800-247-5251.

PECAN PAN-FRIED CHICKEN

6 **skinless, boneless chicken
    breast halves
    Salt and freshly ground
    black pepper**
¾ **cup finely chopped pecans**
¾ **cup all-purpose flour**
1 **tablespoon paprika**
1 **cup buttermilk
    Vegetable oil for frying**

Place 1 chicken breast half at a time between 2 pieces of plastic wrap and gently pound flat with a mallet until the chicken is about ¼ inch thick; season with salt and pepper. Place the pecans on a baking sheet and place under the broiler about 1 to 2 minutes; let cool. Mix the nuts, flour, and paprika in a plastic or brown paper bag. Dip the chicken in the buttermilk, then place in the bag and shake to coat. Shake off any excess flour.

In a 12-inch skillet, heat ½ inch oil over medium-high heat. Add the chicken and cook about 4 to 6 minutes on each side, or until the chicken is golden brown and no longer pink inside.

Serves 6

HERB FRIED CHICKEN

1 **3-pound chicken, cut into**
    serving pieces
1 **cup all-purpose flour**
1 **teaspoon dried sage**
1 **teaspoon dried thyme**
1 **teaspoon dried rosemary**
1 **teaspoon paprika**
1 **teaspoon poultry seasoning**
    Salt and freshly ground
       black pepper to taste
    Vegetable oil for frying

Wash the chicken and pat it dry. In a plastic or brown paper bag, combine the flour, sage, thyme, rosemary, paprika, poultry seasoning, and salt and pepper. Put a few pieces of chicken in the bag and shake to coat. Repeat with the remaining chicken. Shake off any excess flour.

In a 12-inch skillet, heat ½ inch oil to 350°F. Add the chicken, skin side down, and cover. After 5 minutes, uncover; the pan should remain uncovered for the remaining time. After 5 more minutes, turn all the pieces over. Continue cooking for about 10 minutes, or until well browned and crisp and all the juices run clear. Remove the chicken to paper towels. Let sit about 5 minutes and serve.

Serves 4

OVEN-FRIED CHICKEN

1 3-pound chicken, cut into
   serving pieces
   Salt and freshly ground
   black pepper
½ cup White Lily flour
   (see Note)
1 tablespoon Old Bay
   Seasoning
½ tablespoon paprika
¼ cup (½ stick) butter, melted

Preheat the oven to 400°F.

Wash the chicken and pat it dry. Season the chicken with salt and pepper and set aside. In a plastic or brown paper bag, mix the flour, Old Bay Seasoning, and paprika. Pour the melted butter into a 13 × 9 × 2-inch baking pan. Place the chicken, skin side down, in the pan and bake 30 minutes. Turn the chicken and continue cooking 15 to 20 minutes, or until the juices run clear.

Serves 4 to 6

NOTE: I just had to try the White Lily flour on this oven-fried chicken, and it was as good as I thought it would be. You can get it from:

WHITE LILY KITCHENS
P.O. BOX 871
KNOXVILLE, TN 37901

CURRIED FRIED CHICKEN

1 **3-pound chicken, cut into serving pieces**
¼ **teaspoon garlic powder**
¼ **teaspoon onion powder**
1 **teaspoon Lawry's Seasoned Salt**
¼ **teaspoon freshly ground black pepper**
2 **tablespoons curry powder**
1 **cup all-purpose flour**
1 **tablespoon paprika**
   Vegetable or canola oil for frying

Wash the chicken and pat it dry. In a large bowl, combine the chicken, garlic and onion powders, Lawry's Seasoned Salt, black pepper, and curry powder. Rub the seasoning on the chicken with your hands. In a large plastic or brown paper bag, mix the flour and paprika. Put a few pieces of chicken in the bag and shake to coat. Repeat with the remaining chicken. Shake off any excess flour.

In a 12-inch skillet, heat ½ inch of oil to 350°F. Add the chicken, skin side down, and cover. After 5 minutes, uncover; the pan should remain uncovered for the remaining time. After 5 more minutes, turn all the pieces over. Continue cooking about 10 minutes, or until golden brown and the juices run clear. Remove the chicken to paper towels. Let stand 5 minutes and serve.

Serves 4

CORNMEAL OVEN-FRIED CHICKEN

1   **3-pound chicken, cut into
    serving pieces**
½   **cup yellow cornmeal
    Salt and freshly ground
    black pepper to taste**
½   **tablespoon chili powder**
½   **tablespoon dried thyme**
½   **tablespoon dried oregano**
½   **tablespoon dried basil**
2   **tablespoons (¼ stick)
    butter**
3   **tablespoons olive oil**

Preheat the oven to 375°F.

Wash chicken and pat dry. In a large brown paper or plastic bag, mix the cornmeal, salt and pepper, chili powder, thyme, oregano, and basil. Put a few pieces of chicken in the bag and shake to coat. Repeat with the remaining chicken. Shake off any excess coating.

Heat the baking pan in the oven. Add the butter and olive oil to the pan and coat well. Place the chicken, skin side down, on the pan. Bake 30 minutes, then turn the pieces and continue baking 25 to 30 minutes, or until golden brown and the juices run clear.

Serves 6

CHICKEN CROQUETTES

1 **pound diced cooked chicken**
2 **cups cooked yellow rice**
1 **cup green peas**
½ **onion, finely chopped**
2 **teaspoons tomato catsup**
1 **teaspoon Old Bay Seasoning**
2 **eggs, beaten**
1 **cup bread crumbs**
  Vegetable oil for frying

In a large bowl, mix all the ingredients together except the eggs, bread crumbs, and oil. Roll the mixture into small balls, then flatten. Dip into the beaten eggs, then coat in the bread crumbs.

In a large skillet, heat 1 inch of oil to 350°F. Deep-fry the croquettes 4 to 5 minutes, turning once, until they are golden brown. Drain on paper towels.

Serves 6

CHICKEN BREASTS

CHICKEN BREASTS PRIMAVERA

2 **skinless, boneless chicken
   breast halves
   Salt and freshly ground
   black pepper**
¼ **cup diced green bell pepper**
¼ **cup diced red bell pepper**
¼ **cup diced zucchini**
½ **cup sliced mushrooms**
½ **teaspoon finely chopped
   fresh rosemary**
1 **garlic clove, finely chopped**
2 **tablespoons (¼ stick)
   butter**

Preheat the oven to 450°F.

Lightly grease two 12-inch pieces of foil. Place 1 chicken breast half in the center of each. Season with salt and pepper. In a small bowl, mix the bell peppers, zucchini, mushrooms, rosemary, and garlic. Cover the chicken breasts with the vegetable mixture. Add 1 tablespoon of butter to each chicken breast half. Close the foil by bringing 2 edges together and folding down about 3 times. Fold in the ends. Using a sharp knife, make 2 small holes in the top of the foil. Place the packages on a baking sheet and bake 30 minutes, or until the chicken is tender. Use caution when opening.

Serves 2

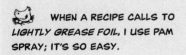

WHEN A RECIPE CALLS TO LIGHTLY GREASE FOIL, I USE PAM SPRAY; IT'S SO EASY.

POTATO HERB CHICKEN BREASTS

2 skinless, boneless chicken
    breast halves
    Salt and freshly ground
    black pepper
1 baking potato, peeled and
    thinly sliced
¼ teaspoon dried thyme or
    ½ teaspoon fresh
¼ teaspoon dried basil or
    ½ teaspoon fresh
¼ teaspoon dried oregano
¼ cup chicken stock

Preheat the oven to 450°F.

Lightly grease two 12-inch pieces of foil. Place 1 chicken breast half in the center of each. Season with salt and pepper. Lay a few potato slices on each chicken breast and sprinkle on the herbs. Drizzle on a little chicken stock. Close the foil by bringing 2 edges together and folding down about 3 times. Fold in the ends. Using a sharp knife, make 2 small holes in the top of the foil. Place the packages on a baking sheet and bake 30 minutes. Use caution when opening.

Serves 2

ORIENT EXPRESS

This quick and healthy weekday dinner is one of my old standbys.
You can easily double or triple the recipe.

2 **skinless, boneless chicken breast halves**
1 **tablespoon soy sauce**
1 **teaspoon dry sherry**
¼ **teaspoon minced fresh ginger**
1 **garlic clove, minced**
1 **scallion, chopped**

Preheat the oven to 450°F. Lightly grease two 12-inch pieces of foil. Place 1 chicken breast half in the center of each. In a small bowl, mix the soy sauce, dry sherry, ginger, garlic, and scallion and pour over the chicken. Close the foil by bringing 2 edges together, folding down about 3 times. Fold in the ends. Using a sharp knife, make 2 small holes in the top of the foil. Place the packages on a baking sheet and bake 30 minutes. Use caution when opening.

Serves 2

CURRIED CHICKEN AND SHRIMP IN A RING

3½ cups cooked yellow rice
(page 51)

1 10-ounce package frozen
green peas and carrots
(see Note)

1½ pounds skinless, boneless
chicken breast, cut into
1-inch pieces
Salt and freshly ground
black pepper

3 tablespoons curry powder

2 tablespoons vegetable oil

1 onion, sliced

2 cups chicken stock

1 pound large shrimp, shelled
and deveined

Mix the rice with the frozen peas and carrots. Grease a 5½-cup ring mold. Lightly pack the rice mixture into the mold, keep warm, and set aside.

Season the chicken with salt and pepper and 1 tablespoon curry powder. Heat the oil in a large skillet over medium-high heat and sauté the onion until translucent. Stir in the remaining 2 tablespoons curry powder and cook a few more minutes. Add the chicken and brown on all sides. Add the chicken stock and bring to a boil; lower the heat and simmer, uncovered, about 15 to 20 minutes, or until the chicken is tender and the curry has thickened. Add the shrimp and cook until pink, about 3 to 5 minutes. Unmold the ring on a platter and pour the chicken and shrimp into the center of the ring.

Serves 6

NOTE: Usually, I cook frozen vegetables according to the directions on the package, but when it comes to frozen green peas or frozen peas and carrots I just put them in a strainer and run very hot water over them for about 3 minutes. Cooking these well makes them too soft, and when you mix them with rice, they won't hold their shape. Just a helpful hint from the Chicken Man!

EASY YELLOW RICE

When I make yellow rice, I just use one packet of Goya Sazón Con Azafrán for each cup of rice and 1¾ cups of water or chicken stock. Most of my friends use turmeric or saffron threads, but I like the flavor I get when I use Goya Sazón Con Azafrán.

CHICKEN CHAMPAGNE

2   tablespoons olive oil
1   tablespoon butter
4   chicken breast halves,
      skinned and boned
    Salt and freshly ground
      black pepper
½   cup all-purpose flour
1   garlic clove, minced
¼   cup chopped onion
1   roasted red pepper, chopped
      (7-ounce jar)
½   cup Champagne
1   10¾-ounce can Campbell's
      Cream of Mushroom Soup
4   cups cooked rice or egg
      noodles

In a 12-inch skillet, heat the oil and butter over medium-high heat. Season the chicken breast halves with salt and pepper to taste. Place the flour in a shallow dish, dip the chicken in, and shake off any excess flour. Add the chicken to the skillet and sauté until brown. Remove the chicken to a plate. Add the garlic, onion, and red pepper to the skillet and sauté about 3 minutes. Pour in the Champagne, stirring up all the pan drippings, then add the cream of mushroom soup. If the mixture is too thick, add a little water. Return the chicken to the skillet, cover, and simmer 25 to 30 minutes, or until the chicken is no longer pink inside. Serve over rice or egg noodles.

Serves 2 to 4

ONION-COVERED EASY CHICKEN BREAST

**2 skinless, boneless chicken
breast halves
Salt and freshly ground
black pepper
3 to 4 tablespoons Homestyle
Sweet Vidalia Onion in
Sauce by Boar's Head
(see Note)**

Preheat the oven to 450°F.

Lightly grease two 12-inch pieces of foil. Place 1 chicken breast in the center of each and season to taste with salt and pepper. Cover the chicken breast with the onions. Close the foil by bringing 2 edges together and folding down about 3 times. Fold in the ends. Using a sharp knife, make 2 small holes in the top of the foil. Place the packages on a baking sheet and bake 30 minutes, or until the chicken is tender. Use caution when opening.

Serves 2

NOTE: Homestyle Sweet Vidalia Onion in Sauce by Boar's Head is available at your local supermarket, but if you can't find it call 1-800-352-6277.

CHICKEN, BLACK BEANS, AND RICE

This is a satisfying dish that I like to prepare when
I'm not trying to whittle down my waistline.

2 **pounds skinless, boneless chicken breasts or thighs**
Salt and freshly ground black pepper
2 **tablespoons vegetable oil**
1 **celery stalk, chopped**
½ **onion, chopped**
1 **garlic clove, minced**
¼ **cup diced red bell pepper**
¼ **cup diced green bell pepper**
½ **jalapeño pepper, finely chopped**
Hot sauce (optional)
1 **15-ounce can black beans, drained and rinsed**
½ **cup chicken stock**
3 **cups cooked rice**
1 **tablespoon chopped fresh cilantro**

Season the chicken with salt and pepper and cut into 1-inch pieces. Heat the oil in a 12-inch nonstick frying pan over medium-high heat. Sauté the chicken for about 20 minutes, or until nicely browned and cooked through; set aside. Add the celery, onion, garlic, bell peppers, and jalapeño pepper to the pan. Sauté about 5 minutes, or until the onion is soft. Stir in hot sauce to taste, if using. Add the black beans and chicken stock. Return the chicken to the pan and cook until the beans are hot. Serve over hot rice and garnish with the cilantro.

Serves 6

NEW YORK-STYLE RICE AND BEANS

I use only cold, leftover rice for this dish. I find that freshly cooked rice turns gummy. My instructor at Queens College, Chef Belinda, turned me on to basmati rice; before that it had always been instant white rice.

3cups cooked basmati rice, cold
1½ cups canned black beans
       (also called turtle beans)
 ½ cup olive oil
1½ onions, finely chopped
1½ green bell peppers, finely
       chopped
5 to 6 garlic cloves, minced
       Hot sauce, to taste

Prepare the rice according to package directions; refrigerate until ready to use. Drain black beans and set aside, but reserve the liquid. Heat the oil in a large cast-iron frying pan over medium-high heat. Add the onions and bell peppers. Cook 5 to 10 minutes, or until the onions are translucent. Add the garlic and cook about 3 minutes more. Stir in the beans and rice. Add the hot sauce and cook until the liquid is reduced, but if too dry add some of the reserved liquid.

Serves 4

HONEY MUSTARD CHICKEN

Triple Sec is an orange-flavored liqueur sold at many liquor stores.
It adds a nice flavor and a little kick to the chicken.

⅓ **cup Dijon mustard**
⅓ **cup honey**
2 **tablespoons chopped fresh dill or 1 tablespoon dried**
2 **teaspoons or more Triple Sec**
4 **skinless, boneless chicken breast halves**

Preheat the oven to 375°F.

Mix the mustard, honey, dill, and Triple Sec in a bowl, then pour into a plastic bag. Add the chicken to the bag and marinate at least 1 hour or overnight in the refrigerator, then place on a lightly greased, foil-lined baking sheet. Bake about 25 to 30 minutes, or until the chicken is no longer pink inside.

Serves 4

CHICKEN THIGHS

BASIL BROILED THIGHS

8 boneless chicken thighs
  Salt and freshly ground
    black pepper
1 tablespoon dried basil
    leaves
1 teaspoon dried oregano
2 garlic cloves, chopped
2 tablespoons dry white wine
⅓ cup olive oil

Wash the chicken and pat it dry. Season with salt and pepper. In a plastic bag, combine the basil, oregano, garlic, wine, and olive oil. Place the thighs in the bag and marinate at least 1 hour or overnight.

Preheat the broiler. Place the chicken, skin side down, on the broiler rack and cook about 6 minutes. Turn and baste with the remaining marinade and continue cooking 10 minutes, or until the juices run clear and the skin is crisp and brown.

Serves 4

TAKING A STAND FOR CHICKEN THIGHS

America, it's time for someone to take a stand for chicken thighs. The chicken thigh is juicier and has more flavor and texture than that breast. You can BAKE, BARBECUE, BROIL, BONE, CASSEROLE, FLATTEN, FRY, KABOB, STEW, STEAM, STIR-FRY, SKIN, STUFF, and ROLL it and the thigh will keep its flavor. Now, I must admit for a long time I was a closet thigh eater, but, America, I'm ready to lead the fight! So come on and drop that breast and grab some thighs.

CHICKEN AND PEPPERS IN A RING

3½ cups cooked white rice
1 10-ounce package frozen green peas (see Note page 50)
4 tablespoons chopped pimiento
2 tablespoons olive oil
1 red bell pepper, cut into strips
1 green bell pepper, cut into strips
1 small onion, thinly sliced
2 garlic cloves, minced
8 skinless, boneless chicken thighs, cut into 1-inch pieces
  Salt and freshly ground black pepper
1 tablespoon red wine vinegar
1 16-ounce can Italian-style stewed tomatoes
2 tablespoons chopped parsley

Mix the rice with the peas and chopped pimiento. Grease a 5½-cup ring mold. Lightly pack the rice mixture into the mold, keep warm, and set aside.

Heat the oil in a large saucepan over medium-high heat. Add the bell peppers, onion, and garlic and sauté about 3 minutes. Remove the bell pepper mixture from the pan. Add the chicken to the pan and brown. Season with salt and pepper, then pour off any fat. Return the peppers to the pan and add the wine vinegar and stewed tomatoes; stir. Lower the heat and cook 20 to 25 minutes, or until the chicken is tender and the liquid has thickened a little. Unmold the ring on a platter and pour the chicken and peppers into the center of the ring. Garnish with the chopped parsley.

Serves 6

MET-CHIP CHICKEN

8 skinless chicken thighs
1 6-ounce bag of Chesapeake
Bay potato chips with crab
seasoning, or any
barbecue-flavored brand
½ cup (1 stick) unsalted
butter, melted
Lawry's Seasoned Salt

Preheat the oven to 400°F.

Wash the chicken, remove and discard the skin, and pat the chicken dry. Line a baking sheet with foil and lightly grease it. In a plastic bag, crush the potato chips to fine crumbs, then pour into a bowl. Pour the melted butter into a separate bowl. Dip the chicken in the butter, then roll in the potato chips. Place the chicken thighs on the baking sheet, leaving space between each. Sprinkle with a little Lawry's Seasoned Salt. Bake about 45 minutes, or until the juices run clear and the chicken is crisp.

Serves 4

CREOLE CHICKEN

2 pounds chicken thighs or
   breasts, skinned and
   boned
   Salt and freshly ground
   black pepper
2 tablespoons olive oil
1 cup chopped onions
1 cup chopped celery
1 cup chopped green bell
   pepper
1 garlic clove, minced
1 bay leaf
½ teaspoon dried basil
½ teaspoon dried thyme
1 8-ounce can tomato sauce
1 cup chicken stock
1 teaspoon hot sauce
1 tablespoon tomato paste
1 10-ounce package frozen
   sliced okra
6 cups cooked white rice

Season the chicken to taste with the salt and pepper. Heat the oil in a porcelain-lined pot or Dutch oven over medium-high heat. Add the chicken and brown on all sides. Remove from the pot and set aside. Pour off all but 2 tablespoons of fat, add the onions, celery, green pepper, and garlic, and sauté about 3 to 5 minutes. Add the bay leaf, basil, thyme, tomato sauce, chicken stock, and hot sauce. Stir in the tomato paste and add the sliced okra. Return the chicken to the pot, cover, and simmer about 25 to 30 minutes, or until the chicken is no longer pink inside. Don't forget to stir occasionally. Serve over hot white rice.

Serves 4 to 6

CAJUN-BARBECUED CHICKEN THIGHS

Recipe phobia? How much easier can it get?

12 **chicken thighs**
⅓ **cup olive oil**
2 **tablespoons McCormick**
Cajun seasoning

Rub the chicken thighs with olive oil and then season with Cajun seasoning. Place the chicken on a preheated grill, bone side down, and cover with foil. Cook 20 minutes. Remove the hood or foil, turn the chicken, and continue cooking about 35 minutes, or until the chicken is brown and the juices run clear.

Serves 4

CHICKEN AND PEPPERS

6 chicken thighs, skinned,
    boned, and sliced
    Salt and freshly ground
    black pepper
2 to 3 tablespoons Crisco Hot &
    Spicy Seasoned vegetable
    oil
2 garlic cloves, chopped
½ green bell pepper, sliced
½ red bell pepper, sliced
½ yellow bell pepper, sliced

Season the chicken with salt and pepper. In a large skillet, heat the oil and sauté the chicken until brown. Add the garlic and sauté about 2 minutes, but do not burn the garlic. Add the peppers and stir well. Cook until the peppers are tender, about 10 minutes.

Serves 4

CHICKEN, GRITS, AND GRAVY

Cooked grits for 4
8 boneless chicken thighs
Salt and freshly ground
black pepper
½ cup all-purpose flour
½ tablespoon paprika
½ teaspoon poultry seasoning
Vegetable oil for frying
½ cup finely chopped green
bell pepper
½ cup finely chopped onion
1 garlic clove, minced
½ celery stalk, finely chopped
2 teaspoons Worcestershire
sauce
1½ cups hot chicken stock

Prepare the grits according to package directions; keep warm.

Place 1 chicken thigh at a time between 2 sheets of plastic wrap and flatten with a meat mallet. Season with salt and pepper; set aside. Combine the flour, paprika, and poultry seasoning in a plastic or brown paper bag, setting aside 2 tablespoons of the seasoned flour. Add the thighs to the bag and shake to coat.

In a 12-inch skillet, heat the oil. Add the chicken, skin side down, and cook, covered, 10 minutes. Uncover, turn the chicken, and cook 10 to 15 minutes, or until the chicken is golden brown. Place the chicken on paper towels. Pour off all but 2 tablespoons of the fat and add the bell pepper, onion, garlic, celery, and Worcestershire sauce. Sauté about 3 minutes, or until the vegetables are soft. Stir in the reserved 2 tablespoons of seasoned flour and cook about 2 minutes, then slowly add the hot chicken stock, constantly stirring until thickened. Return the chicken to the skillet and let simmer about 5 minutes. Put the grits and chicken on a platter and pour the gravy over the grits.

Serves 4

SIMPLE GRILLED THIGHS

Remember when grilling chicken: DO NOT OVERLOAD YOUR GRILL WITH CHARCOAL. The heat will be too high—the outside will be cooked, but the inside will be raw. LOW HEAT = JUICY, TENDER MEAT

10 **chicken thighs**
    Salt and freshly ground
       black pepper
    Paprika
    Onion powder
    Garlic powder
½ **cup (1 stick) unsalted**
       butter, melted with a dash
       or more of hot sauce

Wash the chicken, pat it dry, and season to taste with the salt and pepper, paprika, and onion and garlic powders. Place the chicken thighs on the grill, bone side down, cover, and cook 20 minutes. Turn the chicken, baste with the butter mixture, and cook at least 30 to 35 minutes more, basting and turning until the chicken is done and the juices run clear.

Serves 4 to 6

STOVETOP CHICKEN

MY MOTHER'S FRICASSEE CHICKEN

I remember the wonderful aromas that filled our kitchen on Sunday afternoons as we all sat around the dinner table and my mother made her famous fricassee chicken. Come back to the table—even if it's only a few nights a week. Take the time to enjoy good food and family—these are memories you'll never forget.

1　**3½- to 4-pound stewing chicken, cut into serving pieces**
　Salt and freshly ground black pepper
2　**large onions, sliced**
1½　**cups chicken stock**
1½　**cups water**

Wash the chicken and pat it dry. Season with salt and pepper. Sweat the fowl by placing it in a covered Dutch oven over low heat and simmering about ½ hour. Uncover, add the onions, and brown with the chicken. If too much fat is in the pot after you have sweat and browned the chicken and onions, pour off some. Add the chicken stock and water and bring to a boil; lower the heat to a simmer, cover, and cook about 1 to 1½ hours, or until the chicken is tender.

Serves 4 to 6

SWEET GEORGIA BROWN CHICKEN

1 **3-pound chicken, cut into
    serving pieces
    Salt and freshly ground
    black pepper**
2 **tablespoons (¼ stick)
    unsalted butter**
2½ **tablespoons brown sugar**
1 **onion, sliced**
1 **green bell pepper, sliced**
2 **garlic cloves, minced**
¼ **teaspoon dried thyme**
1½ **cups chicken stock**

Wash the chicken and pat it dry. Season with salt and pepper to taste. Melt the butter in a large skillet over medium-high heat. Add the brown sugar and stir until dissolved. Add the chicken and brown, then stir in the onion, green pepper, garlic, and thyme and cook about 5 minutes, stirring at times. Add the chicken stock and bring to a boil; reduce the heat. Cover and simmer about 20 to 25 minutes, or until the chicken is tender.

Serves 6

CHICKEN GUMBO WITH A LITTLE ZIP

This is nice served with a good crusty bread and a glass of wine.

2 **pounds skinless, boneless chicken breasts, cut into 1-inch pieces**
  Salt and freshly ground black pepper
2 **tablespoons curry powder**
2 **tablespoons (¼ stick) butter or margarine**
1 **tablespoon olive oil**
1 **cup flour**
1 **onion, chopped**
1 **cup chopped celery**
1 **garlic clove, chopped**
½ **teaspoon dried thyme**
½ **cup long-grain rice**
1 **16-ounce can whole tomatoes, chopped**
1 **10-ounce package frozen okra**
1 **bay leaf**
3 **cups chicken stock**
  Hot sauce

Season the chicken with salt and pepper and curry powder. Heat the butter and oil in a Dutch oven over medium-high heat. Pour the flour into a paper or plastic bag. Add a few pieces of the seasoned chicken at a time and shake to coat. Sauté the chicken until brown, then remove from the pot. Add the onion and celery and sauté about 3 minutes, then add the garlic and thyme and sauté 2 minutes more. Add the chicken, rice, tomatoes, okra, and bay leaf.

Add the chicken stock and bring to a boil. Reduce the heat to a simmer and cover. Cook 25 to 30 minutes, or until the chicken and rice are tender. Add hot sauce to taste. Discard the bay leaf before serving.

Serves 4

CHICKEN AND SPAGHETTI

3 pounds skinless, boneless
   chicken breast and/or
   thighs, cut into 1-inch
   chunks
   Salt and freshly ground
   black pepper
3 tablespoons olive oil
1 onion, sliced
2 garlic cloves, minced
1 green bell pepper, sliced
2 yellow bell peppers, sliced
1 28-ounce can whole
   tomatoes, chopped
2 tablespoons tomato paste
¼ cup dry red wine
3 fresh basil leaves, chopped,
   or ½ teaspoon dried basil
½ teaspoon celery salt
1 pound spaghetti, cooked

Season the chicken with salt and pepper. In a large skillet, heat the oil over medium-high heat. Add the chicken and brown on all sides. Remove the chicken and set aside. Pour off all but 2 tablespoons of oil. Add the onion, garlic, and green and yellow peppers and sauté about 3 minutes. Add the tomatoes, tomato paste, wine, basil, and celery salt and bring to a boil. Then lower the heat and simmer, uncovered, about 20 to 25 minutes, or until the chicken is tender. Serve over the cooked spaghetti.

Serves 4 to 6

CHICKEN CHILI

This hearty chili is nice for a big group. Add chips and salsa, a nice green salad, and crusty bread and you have the makings of a Monday night football supper.

2 tablespoons vegetable oil
2 pounds ground chicken
1½ cups chopped onion
1½ cups chopped celery
1 green bell pepper, chopped
2 garlic cloves, minced
1 16-ounce can whole tomatoes, chopped
2 tablespoons tomato paste
1 15-ounce can red kidney beans, drained
1 15-ounce can white kidney beans, drained
1 4-ounce can green chili peppers, chopped
1 1.25-ounce package Durkee chili seasoning
2 cups water
8 cups hot cooked rice

Heat 1 tablespoon oil in a large nonstick skillet over medium-high heat. Add the ground chicken and cook until browned; set aside. Heat the remaining tablespoon of oil in a large Dutch oven over medium-high heat and sauté the onions, celery, bell pepper, and garlic about 5 minutes. Add the cooked ground chicken to the Dutch oven along with the tomatoes and tomato paste; stir. Add the beans, chopped chilies, chili seasoning, and water; stir. Bring to a boil, mix thoroughly, then lower the heat and simmer, uncovered, 25 minutes. Check the seasoning for taste. Serve over hot rice.

Serves 6 to 8

WANDA'S AMAZING CHICKEN

Wanda is married to my co-worker William Bizald. I was at their daughter's birthday party when I tasted this amazing chicken.

1 **3-pound chicken, cut into 12 serving pieces**
2 **0.17-ounce packets of Goya Sazón Con Culantro Y Achiote**
   Salt and freshly ground black pepper to taste
¼ **teaspoon garlic powder**
¼ **teaspoon onion powder**
1 **tablespoon vinegar**
1 **tablespoon vegetable or canola oil, plus additional oil for frying**

Wash the chicken and pat it dry.

Season with Goya Sazón, salt and pepper, garlic and onion powders, vinegar, and 1 tablespoon oil. Place the chicken in a large plastic bag and marinate overnight in the refrigerator.

In a 12-inch skillet, heat ½ inch oil over medium-high heat. Add the chicken, skin side down, and cover. After 5 minutes, uncover; the pan should remain uncovered for the remaining time. After 5 more minutes, turn all the pieces over. Continue cooking for about 10 minutes more, or until crisp and the juices run clear. Remove the chicken to paper towels. Let sit for 5 minutes and serve.

Serves 4 to 6

NUTTY CHICKEN

1 **3-pound chicken, cut into
   serving pieces
   Salt and freshly ground
   black pepper**
½ **cup walnuts or pecans**
1 **cup all-purpose flour**
1 **tablespoon paprika**
½ **cup vegetable oil for frying**
1½ **cups milk**

Preheat the oven to 350°F.

Season the chicken with salt and pepper to taste. Place the nuts on a baking sheet and roast for 10 minutes; let cool, then finely chop. In a plastic or brown paper bag, mix the flour and nuts. Season the flour with ½ teaspoon salt, ½ teaspoon pepper, and the paprika. Reserve 2 tablespoons of seasoned flour. Put a few pieces of chicken in the bag and shake to coat. Repeat with the remaining chicken. Shake off any excess flour.

Heat the oil in a 12-inch skillet and add a few pieces of chicken at a time. Brown the chicken all over, remove from the skillet, and set aside. Pour off all but 2 tablespoons of the pan drippings, mix with the reserved seasoned flour, and stir until it browns. Add the milk and stir until the mixture thickens. Add the chicken, lower the heat, cover, and cook about 25 to 30 minutes, or until the chicken is tender.

Serves 4 to 6

SMOTHERED-WITH-LOVE CHICKEN

I always season my chicken the day before it's time to cook it because then the season-ing has more time to "kiss" the chicken. This dish is great with fluffy mashed potatoes.

1 **3-pound chicken, cut into serving pieces**
  Salt and freshly ground black pepper to taste
¼ **teaspoon onion powder**
¼ **teaspoon garlic powder**
¼ **teaspoon paprika**
½ **cup all-purpose flour**
3 **tablespoons olive oil**
2 **tablespoons (¼ stick) unsalted butter**
1 **onion, sliced**
1½ **cups hot chicken stock**
  Pinch of red pepper flakes

Season the chicken with salt and pepper, onion and garlic powders, and paprika. Dredge the chicken in the flour.

Heat the oil and butter in a 12-inch skillet over medium-high heat. Add the chicken and brown on all sides. When the chicken is browned, remove from the skillet and set aside. Add the onion and sauté until translucent and beginning to brown. Return the chicken to the skillet. Add the hot chicken stock to the skillet just up to side of the chicken and the red pepper. Bring to a boil; lower the heat to a simmer, cover, and cook about 30 to 40 minutes, or until the chicken is tender and the chicken stock has thickened up to the consistency of a gravy.

Serves 4 to 6

CORN BREAD CHICKEN BURGERS
WITH CREOLE MAYONNAISE

⅓ cup corn bread stuffing mix, prepared
1 pound ground chicken
1 large egg
  Salt and freshly ground black pepper to taste
  Dash of hot sauce

CAJUN MAYONNAISE
(for 4 burgers)

¼ cup mayonnaise
1 tablespoon ketchup
2 tablespoons sweet relish
½ tablespoon Creole seasoning, or to taste (see Note)

  Vegetable oil for frying
4 English muffins, split and toasted
4 romaine lettuce leaves
4 tomato slices

Prepare the corn bread stuffing according to package directions. In a large bowl, mix together the stuffing, ground chicken, egg, salt and pepper, and hot sauce. Shape into 4 not-too-thick burgers.

In a small bowl, mix the mayonnaise, ketchup, sweet relish, and Creole seasoning; set aside.

In a nonstick skillet, heat a small amount of oil over medium-high heat. Cook the burgers 6 to 7 minutes per side, until well done. Split and toast the English muffins, spread Cajun mayonnaise on both sides of the muffin, then add the lettuce, burger, and tomato.

Serves 4

VARIATION: ¾ pound ground chicken, and ¼ pound ground pork (2 links of hot or sweet Italian sausage)

NOTE: In the summer of '96, I was in New Orleans at the airport at the end of my trip and picked up Tony Chachere's Creole Seasoning. It's the best. If you can't find it locally, call 1-800-551-9066.

CHICKEN IN WINE

This is one of the first recipes I learned using wine. Chef Roberts told the class the golden rule about using wine when cooking: "If you can't drink it, don't cook with it."

1 **3½- to 4-pound chicken, cut into serving pieces**
   Salt and freshly ground black pepper
2 **tablespoons (¼ stick) butter**
1 **tablespoon olive oil**
1 **tablespoon flour**
1 **cup chicken stock**
2 **cups French Beaujolais wine**
1 **tablespoon chopped fresh tarragon**

Season the chicken with salt and pepper. In a large deep skillet, melt the butter and add the olive oil over medium-high heat. Brown the chicken on all sides, then sprinkle with the flour and stir about 1 to 2 minutes. Pour in the chicken stock and wine, taste for seasoning, and add the tarragon. Bring to a boil, lower the heat, and simmer about 35 to 40 minutes, or until the chicken is tender.

Serves 4

STEWED CHICKEN AND SMALL WHITE BEANS

1 **3-pound chicken, skinned
and cut into serving pieces**
**Salt and freshly ground
black pepper**
1 **celery stalk, chopped**
1 **onion, finely chopped**
1 **green bell pepper, chopped**
2 **cups canned stewed
tomatoes**
3 **cups water or chicken stock**
1 **can small white beans,
drained**

Wash the chicken and pat it dry. Season with salt and pepper. In a large stockpot, place the chicken, celery, onion, green pepper, stewed tomatoes, and water or stock. Bring to a boil. Reduce the heat to low; cover and simmer 40 to 45 minutes, or until the chicken is no longer pink. Add the beans and simmer 5 minutes more, or until the beans are hot. I always let stew or soup cool, then place in the refrigerator for a few hours so I can skim off the fat before reheating.

Serves 6

NEW WORLD CHICKEN

1 **3-pound chicken, cut into
   serving pieces
   Salt and freshly ground
   black pepper**
2 **tablespoons palm oil
   (see Note)**
1 **red onion, sliced**
1 **green bell pepper, cut into
   strips**
2 **tomatoes, peeled and
   chopped**
3 **fresh thyme sprigs**
1 **15-ounce can tomato sauce**

Wash the chicken and pat it dry. Season the chicken to taste with salt and pepper. Heat the palm oil in a 12-inch skillet over medium heat. Add the chicken and sauté about 5 minutes. Remove the chicken from the skillet and set aside. Add the onion, green pepper, tomatoes, and thyme and sauté about 3 to 5 minutes. Add the chicken and tomato sauce; bring to a boil. Reduce to a simmer, cover, and cook 20 to 25 minutes, or until the chicken is tender. Remove the thyme sprigs before serving.

Serves 4

NOTE: Palm oil is available at most African and Asian food markets. This reddish-orange oil has a distinctive flavor that is popular in West African cooking.

COFFEE MAY CHANGE BUT CHICKEN WILL ALWAYS BE THE SAME

In the summer of '96 I started stopping at a coffee shop in the Park Slope section of Brooklyn called New World Coffee. The first day I walked in the aroma just took me away. Espresso Con Panna, Café Romano, Café Latte—I guess I'm a "give me a regular cup of coffee" kind of guy, but after a few weeks I became a fixture in the shop. One morning the manager, Eric Nyarko, said to me, "Why not try something new?" He put me on the spot. I couldn't let him know that I was C.T.I. (Coffee Taste Impaired) so I tried something new and now I'm hooked on that fancy coffee. I guess you are wondering how the chicken fits in. Well, Eric is from West Africa and is a food lover as well, so we came up with this recipe for New World Chicken.

CHICKEN IN A GLASS SITTING ON THE GRASS

This is the dish I wowed my editor with at one of our first meetings.
It is very tasty and makes for a nice presentation.

3 **pounds skinless, boneless**
   chicken, cut into chunks
   Salt and freshly ground
   black pepper
2 **tablespoons vegetable oil**
2 **garlic cloves, minced**
⅔ **cup white wine**
1 **16-ounce can peeled whole**
   tomatoes, chopped
½ **teaspoon dried thyme**
2 **cups cooked yellow rice**
4 **cups cooked collard greens**

Season the chicken chunks with salt and pepper. Heat the oil in a 12-inch skillet over medium-high heat. Add the chicken and garlic and sauté 5 to 10 minutes. Remove the chicken from the skillet and set aside. Discard the fat and deglaze the skillet with the wine. Add the tomatoes and thyme to the skillet. Return the chicken to the skillet and bring to a boil. Reduce the heat to a simmer and cover. Cook about 20 minutes, or until the chicken is tender.

In a tall glass (trifle) bowl with high sides, about 8 inches in diameter, layer the yellow rice, collard greens, and chicken. Pour any remaining tomato sauce on top.

Serves 4 to 6

CHICKEN IN RED GRAVY

1 **3-pound chicken, cut into
   serving pieces
   Salt and freshly ground
   black pepper**
¼ **teaspoon garlic powder**
¼ **teaspoon onion powder**
¼ **teaspoon paprika**
2 **tablespoons vegetable oil**
1 **cup all-purpose flour**
1 **onion, sliced thin**
3 **tablespoons tomato paste
   Pinch of sugar**
2 to 2½ cups hot chicken stock

Wash the chicken and pat it dry. Season with the salt and pepper, garlic and onion powders, and paprika. Heat the oil in a pot over medium-high heat. Dredge the chicken in the flour, shaking off any excess, and brown on all sides. Remove the chicken from the pot and set aside. Add the onion and cook until translucent and soft. Add the tomato paste and sugar and cook 3 minutes, stirring constantly. Return the chicken to the pot and coat with the tomato paste. Add just enough hot chicken stock to almost cover and bring to a boil. Reduce the heat to a simmer, cover, and cook 25 to 30 minutes, or until the chicken is tender.

Serves 4 to 6

CHICKEN SAUSAGE AND PEPPERS

1 pound chicken sausage
2 tablespoons olive oil
1 large onion, sliced
1 green bell pepper, cut into
   strips
1 red bell pepper, cut into
   strips
2 garlic cloves, minced
½ tablespoon dried oregano
½ cup chicken stock
1 tablespoon soy sauce

Place the sausage in a lightly oiled skillet over medium heat. Brown the sausage on all sides. Cover and cook 15 minutes or until sausage is no longer pink in the center. Remove the sausage from the skillet and set aside. Add the olive oil to the skillet and heat over medium-high heat. Add the onion and peppers, and cook about 5 minutes, or until soft. Add the garlic and oregano and sauté 2 minutes more. Cut the sausage diagonally into 1-inch slices and return to the pan. Add the chicken stock and soy sauce and simmer about 10 minutes.

Serves 4

GRILLED AND BROILED CHICKEN

DRUNKEN CHICKEN

I'm always talking to people about chicken and chicken recipes. Sometimes I hear some wild recipes, like this Drunken Chicken—I had to try it right away! There I was in the middle of winter in the backyard with my overcoat, my Weber barbecue pit, one chicken, and one can of beer. But it was worth it; this is one you must try.

1 3-pound whole chicken
3 tablespoons Tony Chachere's Creole Seasoning (see Note page 79)
1 12-ounce can of your favorite beer

Light a fire in a barbecue pit and use the Indirect Cooking Method (see Note). Wash the chicken and pat it dry. Season the chicken inside and out with Tony Chachere's seasoning. Wash the beer can, then open and pour out about 2 ounces. Insert the beer can into the chicken cavity. Carefully place the chicken on the grill; the chicken should be sitting upright and well balanced. Close the lid and open the air holes halfway on the smoker. The cooking time is about 1½ hours. Check the chicken to make sure it has not fallen over. Use tongs to remove the chicken from the grill and also to remove the can from the cavity to prevent burns. Let the chicken rest about 5 minutes before serving.

Serves 6

NOTE: The Indirect Cooking Method requires putting a drip pan at the bottom of the pit, then placing the charcoal around the pan. Cook the meat on the grill over the drip pan.

OVEN DRUNKEN CHICKEN

After cooking this recipe outside, you know I just had to see how it would work in the oven. So here it is. This one is good and juicy, too, but doesn't have that barbecue pit flavor.

1　**3-pound chicken, whole**
2　**tablespoons butter, softened**
3　**tablespoons Tony Chachere's Creole Seasoning (see Note)**
1　**12-ounce can of your favorite beer**

Place your oven rack to the lowest level, then preheat the oven to 375°F.

Wash the chicken and pat it dry. Rub it with butter and then season with Tony Chachere's seasoning inside and out. Wash the beer can, then open and pour out about ⅓ of the beer. Insert the beer can into the cavity of the chicken. Place the chicken sitting upright and well balanced in a roasting pan on the oven rack. Cook about 60 minutes or until the juice runs clear. Use tongs to remove the can from the chicken. There will still be some beer in the can and it will be HOT, so be careful.

Serves 6

NOTE: If you can't find Tony Chachere's Creole Seasoning, call them at 1-800-551-9066.

GRILLED LEMON CHICKEN

When my friend Alicia Thurston made this wooden Chicken Man doll for me,
I had to cook up this delicious dish for her.

1 3-pound chicken, butterflied
1 teaspoon salt
½ teaspoon freshly ground
    black pepper
⅓ cup unsalted butter, melted
2 lemons, juiced
¼ teaspoon hot sauce, or to
    taste
½ tablespoon dried thyme

Wash the chicken and pat it dry. Butterfly the chicken by cutting out the backbone with poultry shears. Turn the chicken breast side up and press flat with the heel of your hand. Season the chicken with the salt and pepper, then place in a wire toaster basket. In a small bowl, mix together the melted butter, lemon juice, hot sauce, and thyme. Grill the chicken over medium-hot coals, basting regularly with the lemon mixture, for about 30 to 45 minutes, or until the chicken is tender and the juices run clear.

Serves 4

GRILLED LIME CHICKEN

1   **3-pound chicken, cut into serving pieces**
½   **cup fresh lime juice**
½   **cup olive oil**
1   **teaspoon salt**
½   **teaspoon freshly ground black pepper**
1   **lime, sliced**
1   **red onion, sliced**
2   **garlic cloves, minced**
1   **teaspoon fresh thyme or ½ teaspoon dried**

LIME BUTTER

½   **cup (1 stick) unsalted butter, softened**
½   **cup fresh lime juice**

Wash the chicken and pat it dry. In a large plastic bag, combine all the ingredients except those for lime butter. Marinate in the refrigerator for at least 3 hours or overnight. In a small bowl, mix the softened butter and lime juice together. Place the mixture on a sheet of wax paper and shape into a cylinder; place in the refrigerator until ready to use. Remove the chicken from the marinade and cook over a medium-hot grill about 35 to 45 minutes, or until the juices run clear. Serve hot with lime butter.

Serves 4 to 6

STEAMED GRILLED BARBECUED DUCK

If you don't have a steamer, take a large stockpot, place a heatproof bowl in the bottom of the pot, and place a plate or rack on it. Add water to just below the plate (making sure not to cover the plate), lay the duck on it, and cover. Cook over medium-high heat.

1 **duck, about 4 pounds**
   Salt and freshly ground
   black pepper
1 **large orange, halved**
   Barbecue sauce

Wash the duck inside and out, pat dry, prick the skin with a fork, and season with salt and pepper. Stuff the duck with the orange halves. Steam the duck about 50 to 55 minutes. Remove the duck from the steamer, discard the orange halves, and wipe off the excess fat with a paper towel. Split the duck, place in a barbecue basket, and grill over medium-high heat about 30 to 35 minutes, turning and basting with the barbecue sauce until the duck is done.

Serves 4

GRILLED CHICKEN WITH GARLIC AND ROSEMARY

1 **3-pound chicken, cut into serving pieces**
4 **garlic cloves, minced**
2 **tablespoons chopped fresh rosemary**
1 **teaspoon salt**
½ **teaspoon freshly ground black pepper**
¼ **cup olive oil**

In a large plastic bag, combine all the ingredients. Marinate 1 hour or in the refrigerator overnight. Place the chicken on a grill over medium-high heat. Cook about 35 to 40 minutes, or until the chicken is no longer pink inside, basting and turning occasionally.

Serves 4 to 6

Which came first ?

The Chicken or the Grill ?

THE RED HENS

A chicken tip: When I barbecue chickens or hens, I use a grill basket because it allows me to turn the chicken or hen all once and it doesn't fall apart. Just before grilling, brush oil on the basket so the chicken doesn't stick to it.

2 Cornish hens
2 tablespoons plain yogurt
**3 tablespoons Patak's Original
     Tandoori Paste**
1 lemon, juiced

Butterfly the Cornish hens by removing the backbone with poultry shears. Place the hens breast side up and flatten them with the heel of your hand. Remove the skin and with a sharp knife, cut diagonal slashes in the meat.

In a small bowl, mix the yogurt and tandoori paste. In a large plastic bag, combine the hens, lemon juice, and yogurt-tandoori mixture. Marinate in the refrigerator for at least 2 to 3 hours or overnight. Place the hens in a wire toaster basket and grill over medium-hot coals about 35 to 40 minutes, turning the basket 2 to 4 times until the hens are done.

Serves 2

CHICKEN AND PORK BURGERS

¾ **pound ground chicken**
¼ **pound ground pork (2 links**
     of Italian sausage)
½ **cup chopped green onions**
 1 **garlic clove, minced**
 1 **teaspoon Worcestershire**
     sauce
    McCormick Cajun Seasoning
     to taste
    Salt and freshly ground
     black pepper to taste

Preheat the broiler or grill. Mix the ground chicken and pork with the green onions, garlic, Worcestershire sauce, Cajun seasoning, and salt and pepper. Shape into 4 not-too-thick burgers. Place the burgers on a broiler pan and cook 6 to 7 minutes on each side, until the burgers are cooked through and spring back to the touch.

Serves 4

HIP-HOP-HOT 97 CHICKEN

4 chicken leg quarters,
   skinned
¾ cup plain yogurt
1 teaspoon salt
2 to 3 chipotle peppers
   (in adobo), chopped
   (see Note)
1 garlic clove, minced

Preheat the broiler.

Remove the skin from the chicken and with a sharp knife cut deep diagonal cuts into the meat. In a small bowl, mix together the yogurt, salt, chipotle pepper, and garlic and brush on the chicken. Cover and refrigerate 2 hours or overnight. Place on the broiler pan about 6 to 7 inches from the heat and cook about 10 minutes, then turn over and continue cooking 10 minutes more, or until the chicken is brown and the juices run clear. Remember to baste the chicken with the remaining yogurt mixture.

Serves 4

NOTE: Chipotle, a hot chili pepper, can be found dried, canned, smoked, and pickled. It's dried by smoking and often canned in adobo sauce. It has a delicious hot and smoky flavor.

WING HUA III BROILED LEMON-GARLIC CHICKEN

6 chicken breasts, deboned
   (see page 6)
2 lemons, juiced
3 garlic cloves, minced
1 teaspoon salt
½ teaspoon freshly ground
   black pepper
¼ cup olive oil
¼ teaspoon curry powder
   Pinch of sugar

Wash the chicken breasts and pat them dry.

In a small bowl, whisk the lemon juice, garlic, salt, pepper, and oil; set aside. In a large plastic bag, combine the chicken breasts and lemon mixture. Marinate in the refrigerator for at least 1 hour or overnight.

Preheat the broiler.

Place the chicken breasts on a broiler pan, sprinkle with a little curry powder and sugar, and cook 6 to 7 inches from the heat, about 8 to 10 minutes per side, or until the chicken is no longer pink inside.

Serves 6

MILL BASIN CHICKEN

2 chickens, 3 to 4 pounds each
3 tablespoons mayonnaise
½ tablespoon salt
½ tablespoon freshly ground
   black pepper
¼ teaspoon onion powder
¼ teaspoon garlic powder
1 teaspoon paprika
½ teaspoon cayenne pepper
2 cups hickory wood chips

Wash the chickens and pat them dry. In a bowl, mix the mayonnaise, salt, pepper, onion and garlic powders, paprika, and cayenne. Rub down the chicken with this mixture. Soak the hickory wood chips in water about 30 minutes to 1 hour and place on hot coals. (I use an electric smoker, so I don't have to replenish the coals.) Smoke the chicken about 1½ to 2 hours, or until the internal temperature of the breast meat hits 180°F.

Serves 8

BAKED CHICKEN

CRISPY CROUTON CHICKEN

*This recipe is a result of a "quick fix" I needed one evening when
some friends dropped by.*

1 **3-pound chicken, cut into
serving pieces**
2 **cups onion-and-garlic-
flavored croutons**
¼ **teaspoon onion powder**
¼ **teaspoon garlic powder**
 **Salt and freshly ground
black pepper to taste**
½ **tablespoon dried parsley**
1 **cup buttermilk**
 Paprika

Preheat the oven to 375°F.

Wash the chicken and pat it dry. Coarsely chop the croutons
in a food processor fitted with a steel blade. In a large plastic
bag, add the chopped croutons, onion and garlic powders, salt
and pepper, and parsley. In a medium bowl, combine the buttermilk and chicken; coat well. Put a few pieces of chicken in the
bag and shake to coat. Repeat with the remaining chicken.
Place the chicken on a lightly greased foil-lined baking sheet.
Sprinkle with a little paprika. Bake 45 minutes, or until golden
brown and the juices run clear.

Serves 4

CHICKEN LOAF

2 pounds ground chicken
1 cup seasoned bread crumbs
1 cup chopped onion
½ cup chopped green or red
  bell pepper
1 egg, beaten
2 teaspoons Worcestershire
  sauce
½ teaspoon salt
¼ teaspoon freshly ground
  black pepper
1 hard-boiled egg
  Ketchup or barbecue sauce

Preheat the oven to 375°F.

In a large bowl, combine all the ingredients except the hard-boiled egg and ketchup or barbecue sauce. Shape into a loaf and place the hard-boiled egg in the center. Place in a greased 8½ × 4-inch loaf pan and bake 45 to 50 minutes. After 35 minutes, spread on 4 tablespoons of ketchup or barbecue sauce and continue cooking for 10 to 15 minutes. A meat thermometer inserted into the loaf should register 160° to 165°F.

Serves 4 to 6

CHICKEN MAN'S BISQUICK CHICKEN

1 **3-pound chicken, cut into
serving pieces**
1 **cup Bisquick all-purpose
baking mix**
1 **tablespoon paprika
Salt and freshly ground
black pepper**
1 **teaspoon garlic powder**
1 **teaspoon onion powder**
2 **tablespoons (¼ stick)
unsalted butter, melted**

Preheat the oven to 425°F.

Wash the chicken and pat it dry. In a large paper or plastic bag, mix the Bisquick, paprika, salt and pepper, and garlic and onion powders. Coat the baking pan with the melted butter.

Put a few pieces of chicken in the bag and shake to coat. Repeat with the remaining chicken. Add the chicken, skin side down, to the baking pan. Bake 30 minutes, then turn the pieces and continue baking 25 to 30 minutes, or until the chicken is golden brown and the juices run clear.

Serves 4

CHICKEN MAN'S OVEN JERK CHICKEN

1 3-pound chicken, skinned
   and cut into serving pieces
   Salt and freshly ground
   black pepper
1 lime, juiced
2 tablespoons Walker's Wood
   jerk seasoning
¼ cup dark rum

Preheat the oven to 350°F.

Wash the chicken and pat it dry. Season with salt, pepper, and lime juice. Place the chicken in a bowl with the jerk seasoning and rum; marinate 1 hour or overnight in the refrigerator. Place the chicken on a baking sheet and cover tightly with foil; bake about 50 minutes, or until most of the juice has evaporated. Remove the foil and let the chicken brown. Chicken should pull away from the bone easily when done.

Serves 4 to 6

OVEN CURRY THAT COOKS IN A HURRY

1 **3-pound chicken, cut into
serving pieces**
   **Salt and freshly ground
black pepper**
¼ **teaspoon cayenne**
2 **tablespoons curry powder**
3 **tablespoons vegetable oil**
1 **onion, chopped**
1 **10-ounce package frozen
green peas**
3 **potatoes, cut into cubes**
2 **cups chicken stock**

Preheat the oven to 350°F.

Wash the chicken and pat it dry. Season the chicken with salt, pepper, cayenne, and 1 teaspoon of curry powder. Put in a plastic bag and let marinate 1 hour or overnight in the refrigerator. Heat the oil in a skillet over medium-high heat and brown the chicken, then place in a Dutch oven. Add the onion and the rest of the curry powder and cook until tender, then add to the Dutch oven. Add the green peas, potatoes, and stock to the Dutch oven. Place a piece of heavy-duty aluminum foil on top of the chicken and put the lid on. Place in the oven and bake about 25 to 30 minutes, or until the chicken and potatoes are tender.

Serves 4 to 6

EASY TANDOORI CHICKEN

1 **3-pound chicken, cut into**
   8 pieces
1 **lemon, juiced**
2 **tablespoons plain yogurt**
3 **tablespoons Patak's Original**
   Tandoori Paste

Preheat the oven to 425°F.

Wash the chicken and pat it dry. Remove the skin. Using a sharp knife, make a few small slits in each piece of chicken; set aside. Place the chicken in a plastic bag and add the lemon juice. In a small bowl, combine the yogurt and tandoori paste, mix well, and add to the chicken. Marinate overnight in the refrigerator. Place the chicken on a lightly greased foil-lined baking pan. Bake 15 minutes, then turn and continue baking for 20 to 25 minutes, or until the juices run clear.

Serves 4

BAKED SAFFRON CHICKEN

The saffron in the Goya seasoning gives this chicken a beautiful golden color.

1 **3-pound chicken, cut into serving pieces**
1 **cup Italian salad dressing**
1 **teaspoon dried basil**
1 **teaspoon dried oregano**
1 **package Goya Sazón Con Azafrán seasoning**
   Pinch of crushed red pepper flakes

Preheat the oven to 350°F.

Wash the chicken and pat it dry. In a large plastic bag, combine the Italian dressing, basil, oregano, Goya Sazón seasoning, and crushed red pepper flakes. Place the chicken in the bag and marinate 1 hour or overnight in the refrigerator. Place the chicken on a baking sheet or baking dish and cover with foil. Bake 20 minutes. Remove the foil and continue baking about 20 to 25 minutes, or until the chicken is tender and the juices run clear.

Serves 4 to 6

JUICY FINGER-LICKIN', SLOW-COOKING, IN-THE-OVEN BARBECUE CHICKEN

SLOW COOKING + LOW HEAT = JUICY TENDER MEAT.

2 **chickens, cut into quarters**
   Salt and freshly ground
   black pepper
2 **cups barbecue sauce**
   (see page 111)

Preheat the oven to 450°F.

Wash the chicken and pat it dry. Season with salt and pepper. Place the chicken in a large baking pan, coat with the barbecue sauce, and let marinate at least 30 minutes or more. Bake uncovered for 10 minutes. Then cover, lower the heat to 250°F., and bake about 1½ hours, basting occasionally.

Serves 8

CHICKEN MAN'S BARBECUE SAUCE

1 10¾-ounce can condensed
  Campbell's tomato soup
2 tablespoons brown sugar
2 teaspoons liquid smoke
1 tablespoon cider vinegar
2 teaspoons Worcestershire
  sauce
½ tablespoon prepared
  mustard
1 teaspoon salt
½ teaspoon freshly ground
  black pepper

Combine all the ingredients in a saucepan. Cover and cook over low heat about 10 minutes, stirring occasionally.

Makes about 1 cup of sauce

LEMON, GARLIC, AND OREGANO CHICKEN

1	**3-pound chicken, split**
1	**lemon**
10	**garlic cloves**
2	**tablespoons olive oil**
¼	**teaspoon freshly ground black pepper, or to taste**
3	**tablespoons dried oregano leaves**

Preheat the oven to 350°F.

Place the chicken, breast side down, on a cutting board with the neck end away from you. Cut from the tail to the neck along one side of the backbone, then cut down the other side of the backbone; remove the backbone. Lay the chicken breast side up and flatten with the heel of your hand. Remove all the skin from the chicken and place the chicken in a plastic bag. Cut the lemon in half and squeeze the juice over the chicken. Let marinate at least 1 hour or overnight in the refrigerator. Remove the chicken from the bag and lay out, breast side up. Using a sharp knife, poke 10 holes in the chicken and stuff with the garlic cloves. Rub with olive oil, sprinkle with a little black pepper, and cover with the oregano. Bake about 50 minutes, or until the chicken is tender and the juices run clear.

Serves 4 to 6

PEACH CHUTNEY–GLAZED HENS

*Chutney is one of my favorite condiments. It is made up of fruit,
vinegar, and spices and it adds a nice taste.*

4 **Cornish game hens**
   Salt and freshly ground
      black pepper
½ **cup (1 stick) unsalted**
      butter, melted
   Paprika
1½ **cups prepared peach**
      chutney (see Note)

Preheat the oven to 375°F.

Wash the hens, dry them, and cut off the wing tips. Season the hens with salt and pepper inside and out. Place the hens breast side down on a baking pan, brush with the melted butter, and bake 20 minutes. Take out and turn the hens, baste with the butter, sprinkle with paprika, and continue baking about 20 minutes. Take out, brush with the peach chutney, and bake 5 to 10 minutes more, or until the hens are golden brown and the juices run clear.

Serves 4

NOTE: Put the chutney in a small bowl, then place in a microwave on high for a few seconds; this will make it easier to brush.

LENNY THE CHICKEN MAN'S BAKED LEMON CHICKEN

1   **3-pound chicken, cut into serving pieces**
½   **cup fresh lemon juice**
1   **teaspoon onion powder**
1   **teaspoon garlic powder**
¼   **teaspoon paprika**
½   **teaspoon dried thyme**
½   **teaspoon salt**
¼   **teaspoon freshly ground black pepper**
1   **teaspoon hot sauce**
½   **cup (1 stick) butter, melted**

Preheat the oven to 400°F.

Wash the chicken and pat it dry. In a large nonreactive bowl, whisk together the lemon juice, onion and garlic powders, paprika, thyme, salt, pepper, and hot sauce. Add the chicken to the bowl, cover, and marinate at least 3 hours or overnight in refrigerator. Place the chicken in a large baking pan and pour the melted butter over the chicken. Bake 10 to 15 minutes, then lower the heat to 350°F. and bake 30 to 35 minutes, or until the chicken is tender and the juices run clear.

Serves 4 to 6

ROASTED CHICKEN

COOL HENS IN JAMAICA

I love foods that have a little kick! This is one of my favorite hot and spicy dishes.

4 **Cornish game hens**
  Salt and freshly ground
    black pepper
3 to 4 **tablespoons Walker's**
    Wood jerk seasoning
⅓ **cup dark rum**
½ **cup (1 stick) unsalted**
    butter, melted
  Paprika

Wash the hens, pat them dry; cut off the wing tips. Place your finger between the skin and meat and loosen the skin around the hen. Season with salt and pepper. In a bowl, mix the jerk seasoning and rum and rub some under and over the skin; massage in well. Then place in a large plastic bag and let marinate overnight in the refrigerator. (When I make this recipe, I marinate the hens for 2 days so the seasoning really penetrates the meat.)

Preheat the oven to 375°F.

Place hens on a rack in a roasting pan and pour about ½ cup water in the bottom of the pan to keep the smoke down. Pour the melted butter over the hens and sprinkle with a little paprika. Roast the hens about 35 to 40 minutes, or until the juices run clear.

Serves 4

ROASTED CHICKEN ON VEGETABLES

1 whole chicken (3 pounds
    or more)
    Salt and freshly ground
    black pepper
¼ teaspoon garlic powder
¼ teaspoon onion powder
¼ teaspoon paprika
2 tablespoons olive oil
2 potatoes, cut into chunks
2 onions, cut into chunks
2 carrots, cut into chunks
1 celery stalk, chopped
2 garlic cloves, minced
¾ cup white wine

Preheat the oven to 375°F.

Wash and season the chicken with salt and pepper, garlic and onion powders, and paprika. Truss the chicken. In a large oven-proof sauté pan, heat the oil over medium-high heat and brown the chicken all over. After the chicken is browned, remove from the pan and pour off some of the fat, then add the vegetables. Add the white wine, then place the chicken on top of the vegetables and roast in the oven about 50 to 55 minutes, or until the chicken is tender and the juices run clear.

Serves 4 to 6

GARLIC ROASTED CHICKEN

1 **3-pound chicken, butterflied**
2 **teaspoons dried thyme or
    1 tablespoon chopped
    fresh**
½ **teaspoon paprika**
3 **garlic cloves, minced
    Salt and freshly ground
    black pepper**
½ **cup (1 stick) unsalted
    butter, melted**

Preheat the oven to 400°F.

Wash the chicken, pat it dry, and butterfly it by removing the backbone and pressing flat (see page 91). Combine the thyme, paprika, garlic, and salt and pepper and rub underneath the skin and all over the chicken. Place on a rack in a roasting pan, pour the melted butter on, and roast, uncovered, about 50 to 55 minutes, or until it is tender and the juices run clear.

Serves 4 to 6

ORANGE ROASTED CHICKEN

1   **3-pound chicken**
¼   **teaspoon salt, or to taste**
¼   **teaspoon freshly ground
      black pepper, or to taste**
2   **oranges**
⅓   **cup unsalted butter, melted**
2   **tablespoons Triple Sec**
½   **teaspoon dried thyme**
½   **teaspoon dried oregano**
½   **teaspoon dried rosemary**
½   **teaspoon dried basil**
2   **scallions, thinly sliced
      Paprika**

Preheat the oven to 375°F.

Wash the chicken, pat it dry, and season with the salt and pepper inside and out. Cut 1 orange in half and stuff the halves inside the chicken. In a small bowl, combine the melted butter, Triple Sec, herbs, and scallions. Place in a roasting pan and pour some of the butter mixture over the chicken; save some for basting. Slice the other orange and arrange the slices on top of the chicken. Sprinkle with paprika and bake 50 to 55 minutes, or until the juices run clear.

Serves 4

HAND-RUBBED ROASTED CHICKEN

*Putting ¼ cup water in a roasting well cuts down on the smoke
when fat drips in the hot pan and keeps the chicken moist.*

1 **3-pound chicken, butterflied**
2 **garlic cloves, minced**
1 **teaspoon paprika**
¼ **teaspoon dried thyme**
¼ **teaspoon dried rosemary**
¼ **teaspoon dried sage**
¼ **teaspoon dried tarragon**
   Salt and pepper to taste
⅛ **teaspoon cayenne**
2 **tablespoons olive oil**

Preheat the oven to 375°F.

Wash the chicken, pat it dry, and butterfly it by removing the backbone and pressing flat (see page 91). In a bowl, combine all the ingredients. Rub the mixture all over the chicken and under the skin. Marinate at least 1 hour or covered overnight in the refrigerator. Place the chicken on a rack in a roasting pan, pour ¼ cup water into the pan, and roast the chicken about 40 to 45 minutes, or until the chicken is tender and the juices run clear. Cut into quarters.

Serves 4

CHICKEN AND POTATOES

1　**tablespoon olive oil**
2　**shallots, finely chopped**
2　**garlic cloves, minced**
3　**sweet potatoes, cut into chunks**
3　**white potatoes, cut into chunks**
1　**3-pound chicken, cut into serving pieces**
　　Salt and freshly ground black pepper
½　**cup dry white wine**
½　**teaspoon chopped fresh thyme**
½　**teaspoon chopped fresh sage**

Preheat the oven to 425°F.

In a small skillet over medium-high heat, add the olive oil, shallots, and garlic, sauté about 3 to 5 minutes, and pour into a heated roasting pan. Mix in the potatoes and chicken pieces and season with salt and pepper. Pour in the wine and sprinkle with chopped fresh herbs. Roast about 1 hour or more, basting several times, until the potatoes are tender, the chicken is brown, and the juices run clear.

Serves 4 to 6

STUFFED CHICKEN

CHICKEN BREASTS STUFFED WITH ASPARAGUS, SUN-DRIED TOMATOES, AND RICE

6 chicken breast halves with
   bone
   Salt and freshly ground
   black pepper
¼ teaspoon garlic powder
¼ teaspoon onion powder
¼ teaspoon paprika
1½ cups cooked yellow rice
6 cooked asparagus stalks,
   chopped into 1½-inch
   pieces
⅓ cup oil-packed sun-dried
   tomatoes, chopped
2 tablespoons (¼ stick)
   unsalted butter, melted

Preheat the oven to 350°F.

Using a sharp knife, carefully cut a pocket in each chicken breast. Season with the salt and pepper, garlic and onion powders, and paprika; set aside. In a separate bowl, combine the yellow rice, asparagus, and sun-dried tomatoes. Divide the mixture into 6 parts. Stuff the pockets in the chicken breasts with the mixture. Place the stuffed chicken in a lightly greased baking dish or pan and pour on a little melted butter. Cover loosely with aluminum foil and bake 30 minutes. Uncover and continue baking for 15 minutes, or until the chicken is golden brown and tender.

Serves 6

CHICKEN STUFFED WITH WILD RICE, COLLARD GREENS, AND SAUSAGE

1   **3-pound chicken, deboned**
½   **teaspoon salt, or to taste**
½   **teaspoon freshly ground**
    black pepper
    Paprika
½   **cup turkey or pork sausage**
1   **cup cooked wild rice**
½   **cup cooked chopped collard**
    greens
    Kitchen string
2   **tablespoons (¼ stick)**
    butter

Preheat the oven to 375°F.

Wash the chicken and pat it dry. Debone the chicken (see page 6), leaving the leg bones intact. Season with the salt, pepper, and paprika.

In a small skillet, cook the sausage, breaking it into pieces as it browns; set aside. Lay the chicken out, skin side down in a baking pan. Layer the rice on, then add the greens, and then cover with the sausage. Fold the leg back to re-form its shape and truss with the kitchen string. Brush the chicken with the melted butter and bake 55 to 60 minutes, basting occasionally, until the chicken is golden brown and tender.

Serves 6 to 8

CHICKEN MAN'S GREENS

The peak season for collards is January through April, but you can find them year-round most places. This delicious veggie tastes like a cross between cabbage and kale.

Salt
4 pounds fresh collard greens
2 cups chicken stock
2 teaspoons or more hot sauce

Fill a large bowl with cold water and add 2 tablespoons salt. Soak the collard greens for a few minutes, then wash each leaf individually under cold running water. Stack the leaves about 6 at a time, roll in a cigar fashion, and cut into ⅛-inch ribbons.

In a large stockpot, combine the greens and chicken stock and bring to a boil. Cover, then reduce to a simmer. Season with salt and hot sauce to taste and cover. Cook about 45 minutes to 1 hour, or until the greens are tender.

Serves 4 to 6

CHICKEN CORDON BLEU ITALIAN STYLE

6 **chicken breast halves,
   skinned and boned**
6 **prosciutto slices**
6 **provolone cheese slices**
3 **eggs, beaten**
4 **cups Italian bread crumbs
   Oil for deep-frying**

Place a chicken breast half between 2 sheets of clear plastic wrap and pound flat with a meat mallet to about ¼ inch thick. Repeat with the remaining chicken breast halves. Lay 1 slice of prosciutto and cheese on each chicken breast half. The slices should stick out when you fold the chicken breast in half. Dip in the eggs; coat well. Dip in the bread crumbs; coat well. Heat the oil in a deep pan to 375°F. and fry the chicken about 5 to 7 minutes, lower the heat, turn the pieces, and cook about 6 minutes more, or until the chicken is cooked through and golden brown.

Serves 6

VARIATION: Smoked ham and Monterey Jack cheese with jalapeño peppers

CHICKEN AND HAM AND CHEESE IN THE RYE

1 3-pound chicken, deboned
¼ teaspoon salt, or to taste
¼ teaspoon freshly ground
    black pepper, or to taste
¼ teaspoon garlic powder
¼ teaspoon onion powder
2 tablespoons olive oil
3 pounds rye dough (from
    your local bakery)
4 cooked ham slices
4 Swiss cheese slices

Preheat the oven to 350°F.

Debone the chicken (see instructions on page 6). Place the chicken between 2 sheets of plastic wrap, flatten with a mallet, and season with the salt, pepper, and garlic and onion powders. Heat the oil in a 12-inch skillet over medium heat. Cook the chicken about 7 to 10 minutes per side, or until golden brown and the juices run clear; set aside and let cool. Cut the rye dough in half and roll into a 12-inch disk on a lightly floured surface. Repeat with the remaining dough. Place 1 disk on a lightly greased baking sheet. Add the chicken, covered with the ham and cheese slices, on top of the disk, then cover with the remaining disk. Press the edges together to seal. Bake 15 to 20 minutes. Let rest 5 minutes, then cut into wedges.

Serves 6

PROSCIUTTO AND PROVOLONE CHICKEN ROLLS

4 **skinless, boneless chicken breast halves**
   Salt and freshly ground black pepper
2 **tablespoons chopped fresh basil**
8 **provolone cheese slices**
8 **prosciutto slices**
3 **tablespoons olive oil**
4 **tablespoons dry white wine**

Preheat the oven to 350°F.

Place a chicken breast half between 2 sheets of plastic wrap and pound to a ¼-inch thickness with a meat mallet. Repeat with the remaining chicken breast halves. Season with salt and pepper and sprinkle with a little fresh basil. Cover each breast with 2 thin slices of cheese and 2 thin slices of prosciutto. Roll up lengthwise, secure with toothpicks, and place in a medium baking dish. Mix the olive oil and wine together, pour over the chicken, and sprinkle the remaining basil on the chicken. Cover with foil and bake 20 minutes. Uncover and baste and cook about 10 more minutes, or until the chicken is tender.

Serves 4

CHICKEN BREASTS MOZZARELLA

This is a great recipe if you are in a hurry. Each time I make it I try a different kind of pasta sauce. I was in the supermarket and saw a jar of Cajun pasta sauce, so I tried it. The sauce was hot and spicy and with the mozzarella cheese on top, it was great!

4 **skinless, boneless chicken breasts**
¼ **teaspoon salt**
¼ **teaspoon freshly ground black pepper**
¼ **teaspoon garlic powder**
2 **eggs, beaten**
½ **cup Italian-style seasoned bread crumbs**
¼ **cup olive or vegetable oil**
1 **26-ounce jar pasta sauce**
1 **8-ounce package shredded mozzarella cheese**

Preheat the broiler.

Place a chicken breast between 2 sheets of clear plastic wrap and gently pound flat with a meat mallet to about ¼ inch thick. Repeat with the remaining breasts. Add the salt, pepper, and garlic powder to the beaten eggs. Dip the chicken in the eggs, then in the bread crumbs. Heat the oil in a skillet and cook the chicken until golden brown and firm, turning once. Place in an ovenproof dish, pour the pasta sauce over, and top with the shredded mozzarella cheese. Heat under the broiler about 4 to 5 inches from the heat until the sauce is hot and the cheese has melted.

Serves 2

JUICY THIGHS

1 10-ounce package frozen
   chopped spinach or
   chopped collard greens
12 skinless, boneless chicken
   thighs
¼ teaspoon salt, or to taste
¼ teaspoon freshly ground
   black pepper, or to taste
12 thin bacon slices
   Butcher twine
3 tablespoons olive oil
13 garlic cloves, minced
⅔ cup dry white wine
1 28-ounce can whole peeled
   tomatoes, chopped
2 teaspoons chopped fresh
   thyme or 1 teaspoon dried
2 teaspoons chopped fresh
   oregano or 1 teaspoon
   dried

Preheat the oven to 350°F.

Cook the spinach or collard greens per package directions; set aside. Place the chicken thighs, one at a time, between 2 sheets of plastic wrap and flatten with a mallet. Season the chicken with the salt and pepper; set aside. Squeeze the liquid from the spinach or collard greens, place 1 to 1½ tablespoons in the center of each thigh, and roll up. Wrap 1 slice of bacon around the thigh and secure with butcher twine. Heat the oil in a 12-inch skillet over medium-high heat. Brown the chicken on all sides, place in a large baking pan, and set aside. Pour off the fat, add the garlic to the pan, and sauté about 3 minutes (don't burn the garlic). Deglaze the pan with the white wine; add the tomatoes, thyme, and oregano and cook about 5 minutes; taste to check the seasoning. Pour the tomato mixture over the chicken and bake 20 to 25 minutes, or until the chicken is tender. Cut off the twine before serving.

Serves 6 to 8

CORN BREAD AND SAUSAGE-STUFFED CHICKEN LEGS

¼ **pound sausage meat**
¼ **cup chopped onion**
¼ **cup chopped celery**
⅓ **cup chicken stock or water**
2 **tablespoons (¼ stick)
   unsalted butter**
1 **cup corn bread stuffing mix**
8 **large chicken legs**
   **Salt and freshly ground
   black pepper**
¼ **teaspoon garlic powder**
¼ **teaspoon onion powder**
   Paprika

Preheat the oven to 375°F.

In a medium saucepan, cook the sausage, breaking it into small pieces as it browns. Drain the fat from the meat. Add the onion and celery and sauté about 3 minutes. Add the chicken stock and butter, bring to a boil, and stir in the corn bread; mix well. Remove from the heat and let cool. Season the chicken legs with salt and pepper, garlic and onion powders, and paprika. Push one finger between the skin and meat of the chicken legs to make a pocket and stuff with 1 to 1½ tablespoons of stuffing. Place on a foil-lined, lightly greased baking sheet and bake 25 to 30 minutes, or until the chicken is browned and the juices run clear.

Serves 4

CHICKEN STUFFED WITH YELLOW RICE AND SHRIMP

1 **3-pound chicken, deboned**
¼ **teaspoon salt, or to taste**
½ **teaspoon freshly ground**
    black pepper, or to taste
    Paprika
¼ **pound fresh shrimp**
    (15 medium shrimp)
1 **tablespoon Old Bay**
    Seasoning
1 **bay leaf**
2 **cups water**
1½ **cups cooked yellow rice**
    Kitchen string
2 **tablespoons (¼ stick)**
    butter, melted

Preheat the oven to 375°F.

Debone the chicken (see page 6), leaving the leg bones intact. Season with the salt, pepper, and paprika. Clean and devein the shrimp; set aside. In a medium pot, add the Old Bay Seasoning and bay leaf to the water. Bring to a boil, add the shrimp, and return to a boil. Reduce the heat to a simmer and cook the shrimp about 2 minutes. Do not overcook. Drain the pot with the shrimp, set aside, and let cool. In a bowl, mix the yellow rice and shrimp. Lay the chicken out, skin side down, add the rice mixture to the center, and fold back to re-form its shape. Truss the chicken with kitchen string. Brush the chicken with melted butter and bake 55 to 60 minutes, basting occasionally, until the chicken is golden brown and tender.

Serves 6 to 8

CHICKEN IN THE SAND

1 **3-pound chicken, deboned**
   Salt and freshly ground
      black pepper to taste
2 **tablespoons olive oil**
½ **green bell pepper, cut into**
      strips
½ **red bell pepper, cut into**
      strips
½ **onion, sliced**
1 **garlic clove, minced**
½ **teaspoon dried oregano**
½ **teaspoon dried rosemary**
2 **pounds wheat dough**
      (from your local bakery)

Preheat the oven to 350°F.

Debone the chicken (see instructions on page 6). Place the chicken between 2 sheets of plastic wrap and flatten with a mallet. Season with salt and pepper. Heat the oil in a 12-inch skillet over medium-high heat. Cook the chicken about 7 to 10 minutes per side, or until golden brown and the juices run clear. Set aside and let cool. In the same skillet, sauté the green and red peppers, onion, garlic, oregano, and rosemary about 10 minutes; set aside. Cut the dough in half and roll into a 12-inch disk on a lightly floured surface. Repeat with the remaining dough. Place 1 disk on a lightly greased baking sheet. Layer the chicken, then pepper mixture on top of the disk. Cover with the remaining disk, pressing the edges together to seal. Bake 15 to 20 minutes. Let rest 5 minutes, then cut into wedges.

Serves 6

CHICKEN PIZZA UNDERCOVER

You can buy pizza dough at the supermarket or from your local pizzeria.

1 **3-pound chicken, deboned**
½ **teaspoon salt, or to taste**
¼ **teaspoon freshly ground**
   black pepper, or to taste
2 **tablespoons olive oil**
3 **pounds pizza dough**
1½ **cups pizza sauce**
1 **cup shredded mozzarella**
   cheese

Preheat the oven to 350°F.

Debone the chicken (see instructions on page 6). Place the chicken between 2 sheets of plastic wrap and flatten with a mallet. Season with the salt and pepper. Heat the oil in a 12-inch skillet over medium-high heat. Cook the chicken about 7 to 10 minutes per side, or until golden brown and the juices run clear. Set the chicken aside and let cool. Cut the pizza dough in half and roll into a 12-inch disk on a lightly floured surface. Repeat with the remaining dough. Place one disk on a lightly greased baking sheet. Add the chicken, pizza sauce, and mozzarella cheese. Cover with remaining disk, pressing the edges together to seal. Bake 15 to 20 minutes. Let rest 5 minutes, then cut into wedges.

Serves 6

CHICKEN BREASTS STUFFED
WITH SPINACH AND MUSHROOM

4 **chicken breast halves with bone**
Salt and freshly ground black pepper
¼ **teaspoon onion powder**
¼ **teaspoon garlic powder**
¼ **teaspoon paprika**
2 **tablespoons olive oil**
½ **onion, sliced**
1 **garlic clove, minced**
1 **10-ounce package fresh mushrooms, sliced**
1 **10-ounce package fresh spinach, chopped**
1 **tablespoon soy sauce**
2 **tablespoons (¼ stick) unsalted butter, melted**

Preheat the oven to 350°F.

Using a sharp knife, carefully cut a pocket in each chicken breast. Season with salt and pepper, onion and garlic powders, and paprika; set aside. Heat the oil in a 12-inch skillet over medium-high heat. Cook the onion until soft and translucent. Add the garlic and mushrooms and cook about 3 minutes more. Add the spinach and soy sauce and cook until the spinach is wilted; remove from the heat, set aside, and let cool. Divide the mixture into 4 parts. Stuff the pockets in the chicken breasts with the spinach mixture. Place in a lightly greased baking dish and brush with the melted butter. Cover loosely with aluminum foil and bake 30 minutes. Uncover and continue baking for 15 minutes, or until the chicken is golden brown and tender.

Serves 4

STUFFED CORNISH HENS WITH BACON ON THEIR BACKS

4 **Cornish game hens**
Salt and freshly ground
black pepper
1 **tablespoon paprika**
2½ **cups Stove Top Stuffing**
1 **cup cooked pork sausage,**
drained and crumbled
8 **hickory-flavored bacon**
slices
Kitchen string

Preheat the oven to 350°F.

Wash the hens and pat them dry. Season the hens inside and out with salt, pepper, and paprika. Prepare the stuffing according to package directions. Add the sausage and let cool before stuffing the hens. **Do not overstuff.** Wrap each hen with 2 slices of bacon and tie with kitchen string. Place the hens on a baking sheet, breast side down, and bake about 15 minutes. Then turn over, baste the hens, and continue baking about 30 to 35 minutes, or until golden brown and the juices run clear.

Serves 4

BIG BIRD FOR DINNER

Sometimes it's not how fast you get there, but what you do along the way.
Like preparing a nice, slow-roasting chicken because when it's done, you're there.

1 **whole 5- to 6-pound roasting chicken**
  Salt and pepper to taste
1 **large onion, quartered**
1 **celery stalk, chopped**
2 **garlic cloves, minced**
1 **tablespoon chopped fresh sage**
1 **tablespoon chopped fresh rosemary**

RUB MIX

2 **tablespoons (¼ stick) butter, softened**
1 **tablespoon chopped fresh rosemary**
1 **garlic clove, minced**

Preheat the oven to 325°F.

Wash the chicken and pat it dry. Season it inside and out with salt and pepper. Stuff with the onion, celery, garlic, sage, and rosemary.

Then mix the butter, 1 tablespoon rosemary, and garlic together and rub under the skin and all over the chicken. Place on a V-shaped rack in a roasting pan. Roast the uncovered chicken about 1¾ to 2½ hours, or until the juices run clear and a meat thermometer registers 180° to 185° F.

Serves 8 to 10

INDEX